the SEVEN WONDERS *of the* ANCIENT WORLD

SEVEN WONDERS *of the* ANCIENT WORLD

PAUL JORDAN

PEARSON EDUCATION LIMITED

Head Office:
Edinburgh Gate
Harlow CM20 2JE
Tel: +44 (0)1279 623623
Fax: +44 (0)1279 431059

London Office:
128 Long Acre
London WC2E 9AN
Tel: +44 (0)20 7447 2000
Fax: +44 (0)20 7240 5771
Websites: www.history-minds.com
www.pearson educ.com

First published in Great Britain in 2002

ISBN 0 582 77187 0

British Library Cataloguing in Publication Data
A CIP catalogue record for this book can be obtained from the British Library

Library of Congress Cataloging in Publication Data
A CIP catalog record for this book can be obtained from the Library of Congress

10 9 8 7 6 5 4 3 2 1

Typeset by Fakenham Photosetting Limited, Fakenham, Norfolk
Printed and bound in China

The Publishers' policy is to use paper manufactured from sustainable forests.

For Marie

CONTENTS

ACKNOWLEDGEMENTS

The author and publisher would like to thank Julian Smith, classics mentor, for his many helpful contributions and Mac Dowdy, architectural historian, for his careful yet striking reconstructions of the Seven Wonders.

The watercolour paintings appearing in colour throughout originally appeared in J. A. Hammerton, *Wonders of the Past*, 1924.

INTRODUCTIONS

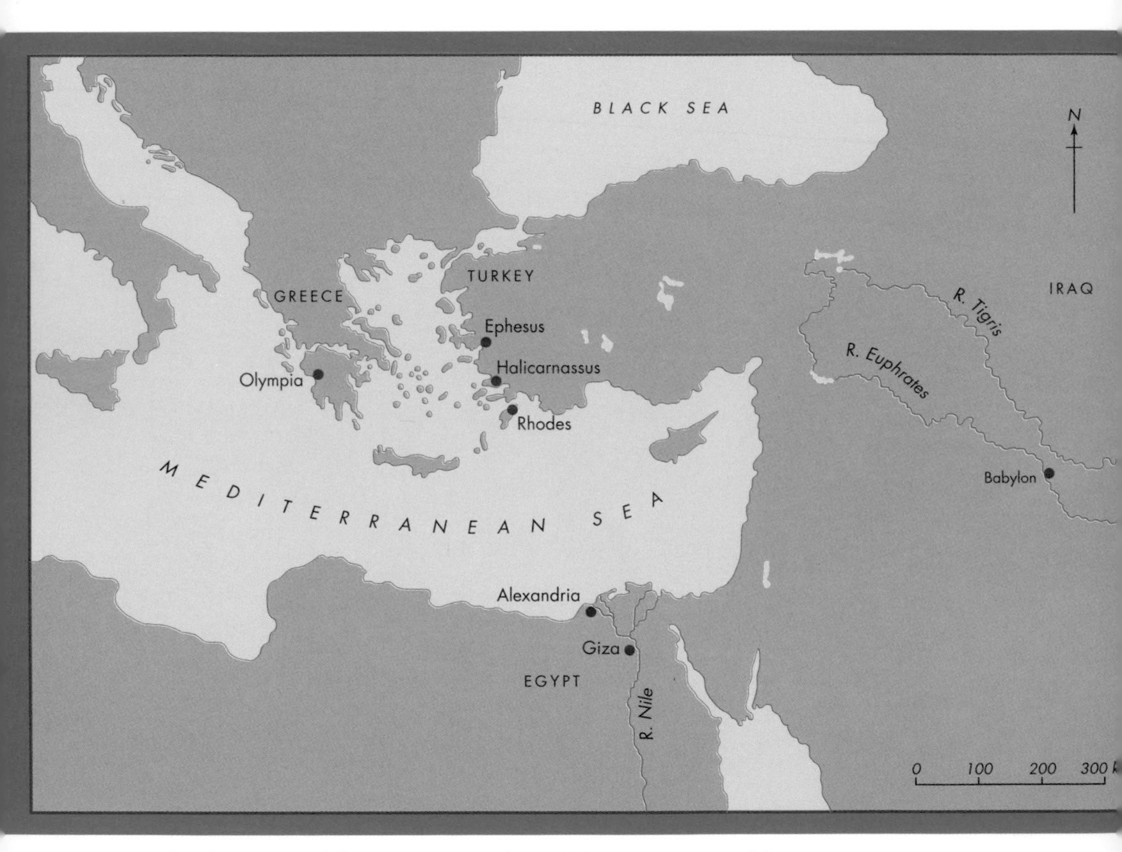

The locations of the Seven Wonders of the Ancient World

Chapter 1
INTRODUCTIONS

THE very notion of The Seven Wonders of the Ancient World raises questions for both of its nouns and both of their adjectives. Why seven? What was so wonderful about these particular wonders? What do we mean by the Ancient World – ancient for whom and what sort of world?

Interestingly, the notion did not start with Wonders but with Sights. The two words in Greek were quite similar and the one slipped into the other naturally enough: theamata turned into thaumata. These Seven Sights – for the armchair travellers of the Hellenistic and Roman worlds to sight-see as they read about them – had to be, in the nature of things, wonderful enough to arouse awe in the first place. On the whole, it was scale of engineering and/or luxury of concept and appointment that prompted the choice. The Pyramids of Egypt had both – unparalleled scale and a seemingly over-luxuriant expenditure of effort to construct them. The Hanging Gardens of Babylon were self-evidently a luxurious indulgence achieved by triumphs of engineering (which were equally apparent in the great walls of that city). The gigantic Statue of Zeus at Olympia was decked in the most elaborate

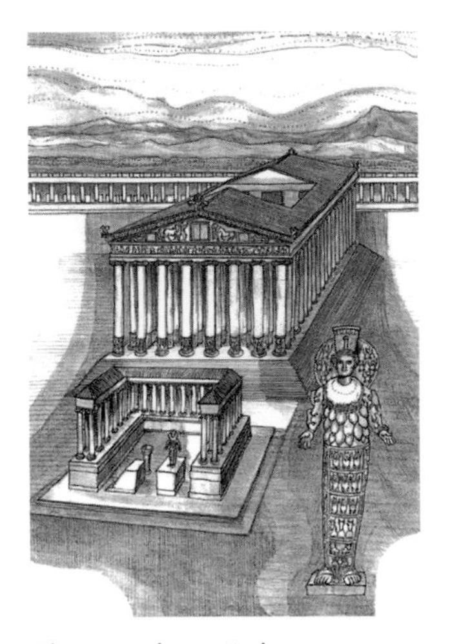
The temple at Ephesus

adornment and sculpted by the most ingenious means. The Temple of Artemis at Ephesus combined scale with vivacity of decoration and pioneering architectural devices. The Mausoleum at Halicarnassus was the biggest tomb in the Graeco-Roman world (after the Pyramids) and exhibited an ostentatious compendium of international styles put together with massive engineering effort. The Colossus of Rhodes, even in the wrecked state into which it fell within half a century of its completion, continued to proclaim the majesty of its conception and ambition of its construction as a ruin. The Pharos lighthouse of Alexandria was before all else an essay in innovatory engineering on a grand scale.

Greatness of size, luxury of appointment and boldness of concept and execution, combining to make a vivid imaginative impact on those who saw them and those who read about them: these were the qualities that first got these sights-cum-wonders listed, in a certain cultural context that we call the Hellenistic world. The same qualities went on recommending them to the Roman world that succeeded and absorbed the Hellenistic one. (With the end of the Roman empire, there came also the end of the entire epoch that we know as 'the Ancient World', reaching back beyond Hellenism through classical Greek and biblical times to the older civilisations of Egypt and Mesopotamia whose first rise marked the beginnings of 'ancient history' for the Western world.)

Hellenism was the international culture that Alexander's conquests of the late fourth century BCE engendered in Greece, in the (mostly eastern) Mediterranean world of Greek colonies and in the Greek-ruled reaches of Egypt and Asia Minor (and some way beyond). Hellenism spoke Greek and read Greek and was heir to the religious, artistic and intellectual traditions of the classical Greeks; but it encompassed, too, the rougher ways of the Macedonian Greeks from whom Alexander the Great himself had sprung and the frankly oriental habits of the peoples brought into the fold in the east. (Alexander, for one, liked to dress up as a Persian and to put on the semi-divine pretensions of the eastern monarchies.) Hellenism survived the political break-up of Alexander's empire at the hands of his succeeding generals and thrived in the cities they maintained, to greatly influence the Roman empire in due course.

Of course, Hellenism did not come into being overnight with Alexander of Macedon. Many of the seeds of its flowering were germinating in late classical Greece. With its trading depots in Egypt and its important commercial cities along the coast of Anatolia, Greece had long been on the receiving end of exotic influences; in some of its richer colonies, in the western Mediterranean too, Greek culture had already taken a turn for the luxurious and even megalomaniac before the coming of the Macedonians in the late fourth century BCE. (BCE = Before the Common Era; CE = the Common Era of our present dating system.)

The philosopher Plato who died in 347 BCE, a decade after Alexander was born, could evidently see the Hellenistic way of life coming in his own day. His moral tale of Atlantis, one of the last things he wrote, was designed to contrast the old, sober virtues of the Greeks (as he saw them) with a changing world's new and luxurious vices, which he projected backwards in time onto his Atlanteans. These Atlanteans finally took grandeur, including self-aggrandisement, luxurious excess and high-handed ambition so far that, for all their power, they were defeated – thousands of years ago in Plato's fiction – by the virtuous Athenians of yore, and then drowned by the gods. Plato might have welcomed the Macedonians at first as a stern, firm hand on the degenerating Greeks around him: he would have been appalled to find Alexander going on to usher in a semi-oriental empire of greedy commerce, ostentation, showy mixed-up religions and everybody on the make. It is to be very much doubted whether he would have been at all impressed with the Seven Wonders of the World that Hellenistic culture was to make so much of.

One of the bonuses of Hellenism was the growth of a sort of university ethos that saw, in the institutions of museums and libraries, the coming-together of scholars to survey and catalogue the achievements of their forerunners in the Greek world and among the non-Greek communities now under Greek influence. Books, above all, were collected, copied, studied, quoted and plagiarised: and it was in the great modern city that Alexander founded on the Delta coast of Egypt that all this went on most famously. Alexandria was the intellectual hub of the Hellenistic ancient world and it was very likely where the Seven Wonders of that world were first listed in the second century BCE.

But all seven (or more) of them were known about before ever they were brought together on any list of the second century BCE. The Zeus statue was on the Greek mainland itself (and the most westerly of the sights). The temple at Ephesus, the Mausoleum and the Colossus of Rhodes were more or less on a line down the south-west coast of Anatolia, long inhabited by Greeks. If you extended that line south across the Mediterranean you reached the Greek city of Alexandria itself where the Pharos beamed its light to incoming ships. Further south in Egypt there were the unmissable pyramids by Memphis, well-known to the Greeks for hundreds of years. Furthest away to the east from the Mediterranean world was Babylon on the Euphrates, where Alexander had died in 323 BCE, long familiar to the Greeks in the works of the historian and travel writer Herodotus. It wasn't knowledge of these various sights that was new in the second century BCE: it was just that the idea of singling them out for their grandeur and magnificence and writing them up on a list was a typically Hellenistic venture. (Herodotus had already written of the 'three greatest works' of the Greeks, all of them – a tunnel, a jetty and a temple – on the island of Samos, as it hap-

The Mausoleum

pened: the naming of wonders was in the air even in the fifth century BCE.)

The world of Hellenism was, of course, but a small part in reality of the diverse doings of human beings on our Earth in the last centuries before the Common Era. Outside the Mediterranean region and its immediate hinterlands – except down into Egypt and towards the east where Alexander's army had reached as far as the Indus and there were established trade routes to modern-day Afghanistan – little was known of the wider world. A few travellers brought back tales of remoter parts, often more or less incredible, with a seepage of similarly unreliable anecdotes from trader to trader across vast lines of exchange that might throw some sort of light on, say, north-west Europe or Africa beyond Egypt or the plains of Asia or distant China. But worthwhile knowledge of these areas was largely unavailable, and completely so as far as vast tracts like the Americas and Australasia were concerned, whose very existence was unknown to the Hellenistic world. What sights and wonders might the compilers of the wonder lists have considered for inclusion if they had known more about the whole wide world of which they formed a small part? They would, no doubt, have applied their fashionable tests for scale and ambition to any far-flung wonders that came their way – and in due course we shall look at the available candidates, on a contemporary global basis, to rival each of the standard seven wonders in turn.

It has been said that in Hellenism we see the first light of our own modern world, with its large-scale political organisation, its vigorous commerce with money in coinage and an international language written in an easily learned alphabet, its town planning, its confidence in technology (up to a point), its cosmopolitan culture, its multi-ethnic urbanisation, its religious relativism, its professionalism and institutionalising of scholarship. All this is often persuasive, but it pays to remember that the past is indeed always a foreign country and they do things differently there. Religion, science, engineering, scholarship were all conducted on the basis

The Hanging Gardens

of quite different assumptions from those we take for granted now, in a world of often very different social relations, of which the existence of slavery is the most glaring example. The Greeks themselves had to recognise this inevitable difference of the past when they looked back to the scarcely believable creation of such wonders as the Pyramids of Egypt or the Hanging Gardens of Babylon and we must remember how different a world it was from our own that created the great cult statue of Zeus at Olympia or the temple at Ephesus with its grotesquely many-breasted goddess or the overblown tomb of Mausolus or the colossal statue of the sun-god at Rhodes. Only the Pharos, the last wonder to join the list, looks altogether like something we might have wanted to create in our modern Western world. Let's hope future generations will look back on our own works with an understanding eye.

We know that in the library of Alexandria at around 270 BCE the scholar-poet Callimachus of Cyrene wrote a book called *Curiosities from All over the World* which reflected, perhaps established, the idea of cataloguing wonderful things, but this work has not survived and evidently did not restrict itself to seven most wonderful of wonders. The first records we have of the practice of listing seven sights and wonders as such belong to the second century BCE. The so-called *Laterculi Alexandrini* and the collection of poetic fragments known as the *Palatine Anthology* both include reference to such lists. In the latter, the epigrammatist Antipater of Sidon (mainly a composer of funeral verses who spent his last years in Rome, dying a drunk there according to one account) is credited with a list very close to the one with which we are all now familiar. It differs only in making two entries for Babylon – the city walls as well as the gardens – and leaving out the Pharos. Something of its poetry comes through even in translation. 'I've looked on the walls of impregnable Babylon, which chariots may race along, and on Zeus beside the river Alpheus. I've seen the Hanging Gardens and the Colossus Sun-God, the great man-made mountains of the tall Pyramids, and the gigantic tomb of Mausolus. But when I saw the sacred home of Artemis that reaches up to the clouds, the others were put in the shade for the Sun has never seen its equal outside of Heaven.' It is interesting that the one wonder that on paper seems the least exciting to us (we all know what Greek temples were like, don't we?) should have aroused the greatest admiration at the launch of the Seven Wonders of the World.

The statue of Zeus

The idea of a list of seven wonders probably took hold quite quickly after the time of Antipater, though its precise items may very well have been a bit changeable from the start. But we don't know for sure that this listing by seven was popularly established until the last days of the Roman republic, in the time of Julius Caesar. Diodorus Siculus, who wrote an anthology of world history in the second half of the first century BCE, records that an obelisk of the legendary Babylonian queen Semiramis ought to be on any list of seven great works. In a piece attributed, probably wrongly, to the Roman librarian Hyginus, of about the same time, the Palace of Cyrus at Ecbatana (further east than Babylon) ousts the Hanging Gardens of Antipater. And Strabo only a few years later, who wrote on historical and geographical themes, mentions the idea of seven sights, among them the pyramids. He does describe among other remarkable things the statue of Zeus at Olympia in the course of his geographical/historical *tour d'horizon*, but not specifically as one of any canon of seven. The list's existence is hinted at by the Latin poet Propertius at about the same time: he would like to think his poetry will prove more endurable than the Pyramids, the Zeus temple and the Mausoleum. In the first century of the Common Era, the 'natural historian' Pliny and the poet Martial similarly attest to some practice of wonder-listing, though with novelties like the Labyrinth of Thebes in Egypt (actually the ruins of the great temple complexes there), the Colosseum in Rome and the Altar of Horns on the island of Delos among their sights worth seeing. Also featuring at various times in various authors' works were the Asclepium (temple-cum-hospital) of Pergamum, and the Capitol of Rome.

It may be that Antipater's original list (without the Pharos and with two sights for Babylon) went on as the most popular listing: a work that poses as a product of the Alexandrian engineer Philo (who lived at about the same time as Antipater) repeats his catalogue precisely, but apparently at a much later date. The real Philo ('of Byzantium', as we know him in full) wrote a *Mechanical Handbook*, which survives in part to reveal itself as mostly concerned with siege engines and defensive devices. The bogus Philo seems to have listed his seven sights in the fourth century CE, but the first report of his list comes in a ninth century manuscript. On the grounds, chiefly, of this Philo's florid and theologically imaginative style in discussing his seven sights, classical scholars dissociate him from the sober, practical engineer of Alexandria in the second century BCE. Of course, the fourth century impersonator of Philo may simply have been giving himself historical credibility by reproducing old Antipater's list.

The Pharos, although discussed by earlier writers like Pliny, only made it onto the lists with Gregory of Tours (536–594 CE), who like other Christian authors shied away from some of the old pagan entries like the Zeus and Artemis monuments – they at least had the merit of having existed – in favour of things like Noah's Ark and the Temple of Solomon, of which the same cannot be said. This difference of approach to the drawing up of wonder lists tells us a lot about the intellectual divergence of the Christian from the Ancient World. The situation with the various listings also reminds us that our modern canon of the Seven

Wonders of the Ancient World is as much the product of recent convention as of some fixed listing in the ancient world itself. True, Antipater more than two thousand years ago advertised a list very close to our own, but the Pharos wasn't on it (and, as we shall see, the Hanging Gardens perhaps shouldn't have been). Our Seven Wonders of the World are really an imaginative composite of ancient wonders, fixed now by long usage since the Renaissance revival of interest in the classical world.

Why were seven wonders listed from at least the second century BCE? For the same reason, essentially, as there are seven days of the week. And, mythologically, Seven Days of Creation, Seven Heavens, Seven Against Thebes, Seven Japanese Gods of Luck, or Seven Wise Men of Greece, Seven Virtues, Seven Chinese Sages of the Bamboo Grove, Seven Deadly Sins, etc. etc. For the same reason, too (though it all looks more everyday), that there are Seven Hills – and churches – of Rome, Seven Senses, Seven Ages of Man, Seven Seas, Seven Planets, even Seven Dials in Holborn and Seven Sisters along the South Downs. Human beings have come to love the number seven – perhaps it even has some neurological appeal. At all events, the Babylonians of the first millennium BCE esteemed this number highly and passed their enthusiasm on to the compilers of the Hebrew Bible; and to Greek thinkers like Pythagoras of the late sixth century BCE, whose followers made much of this number in their influential mathematico-mystic system. Seven was seen as a perfect number of anything to have. And so, Seven Wonders, Seven Sights; even if they were not always the same seven as have come through to us.

Two of the seven wonders were actual products of the Hellenistic world: the Colossus of Rhodes, which may have been idealistically modelled on Alexander himself, and the Pharos of Alexandria. The tomb of Mausolus at Halicarnassus was made for what we might call a small-time precursor of Alexander in a context that immediately predates Hellenism. The temple of Artemis was rebuilt just before Hellenistic times, though a rather older Greek-

The Colossus of Rhodes

style temple had stood on this ancient cultic site. The statue to Zeus at Olympia was a pre-Hellenistic but wholly Greek creation, of the (late) classical heyday. Only the Hanging Gardens of Babylon and the Pyramids of Egypt were altogether non-Greek and pretty much pre-Greek constructions, at least pre-classical Greek in the case of the gardens and wholly pre-Greek in the case of the pyramids. (The Greeks tended – rightly – to credit the Egyptians with a venerably extended antiquity in comparison with their own.)

So it is clear that Hellenistic (and Roman) taste ran to pleasure in sights and wonders that pre-dated their own culture and, in two cases, belonged to older cultures quite alien to their own. They would surely have appreciated many another wonder of the wide world of their day if they had known more of the globe than they could know at the time. Of the peoples who were incorporated into the Hellenistic sphere, the Greeks (including the Macedonians) and the Persians were evidently quite closely related: they belonged to the same broad language group we call Indo-European, as indeed did the Romans and most of the peoples they conquered in western Europe. Indo-European speakers were also to be found across in northern India, where Alexander's army finally stopped its eastward march. In the region across from the Levant to Mesopotamia there were various speakers of the Semitic family of languages – the Babylonians among them, who were credited with the Hanging Gardens. In Egypt, a language of largely Semitic but also partly North African, Berber-related character was spoken: it was an older version of this Egyptian language that had been spoken by the builders of the Pyramids more than two thousand years before Greek-speakers in Alexandria wrote up their wonder-lists; educated Egyptians of Graeco-Roman times could still read the writings of the pyramid age rather as (some) educated English-speaking people today can still read Chaucer.

The Pyramids of Egypt were by far the oldest of the wonders celebrated by the Graeco-Roman world, and though archaeology was an unknown science and knowledge of ancient history was very patchy and garbled, the Greeks and Romans were well aware of Egypt's great antiquity. Indeed they tended to exaggerate it, and to undervalue the longevity of the Mesopotamian continuum of civilisations (of which the wonders of Babylon were a late manifestation). As to the origins of these early civilisations and what might have gone before them, the Greeks and Romans – like all other cultures before our own with our detailed knowledge of archaeology and biological evolution – could only speculate. Plato conjectured that all human prehistory, over an indefinitely long span, had witnessed an endless succession of cycles of rising and falling cities and peoples, with man-made and natural (or divinely ordained) calamities to see off the old and usher in the new, time and time again. It was a reasonable conclusion in the circumstances. It filled infinite time with detailed change in a way that left the whole process always looking in general pretty much the same. Before the concepts of cosmic and biological evolution were compelled by evidence from physics, geology and natural history, Plato's notion was as good as a scientific outlook could hope to achieve. (Later thinkers of the Graeco-Roman world, like Lucretius in the first century BCE, came occasionally close to evolutionary insight.)

The Pyramids at Giza

The Greeks and Romans could not know that we are descended from a common ancestor with the chimpanzees and gorillas of about seven million years ago and that like all the rest of nature we have evolved in accordance with the principles of random mutation and natural selection. The accumulation of adaptive changes, often small in themselves, produced a succession of ancestral forms of humanity able to exploit new niches in the environment by better and better adaptation to the possibilities those niches offered. Bipedal locomotion on two legs, living more and more out of the shrinking forests of Africa, is well attested by some four million years ago. Mental improvement was naturally selected for its survival benefits when toolmaking (and with it almost certainly the beginnings of speech) was developed around two-and-a-half million years ago. Human beings of our own sort of stature and physique (below the neck) had spread beyond Africa by a million years ago, with ever improving stone tool kits and food-procuring strategies, as well as the capacity to make and control fire and furnish themselves with shelter. Their brains show a progressive enlargement over the hundreds of millennia of our evolution. Something more and more like our own consciousness of ourselves and the world about us evolved in concert with those enlarging brains, until by about 35,000 years ago human beings to all intents and purposes just like ourselves had emerged. To the extent that in some places they began to create works of art – wall paintings, engravings, carvings and modellings – that stand up with anything our species has ever produced in this line. If the Alexandrians of the latter half of the second century BCE could have known about them, they might have been tempted to include the painted caves of Lascaux in France and Altamira in Spain among the Wonders of the World.

The creators of these ice age wonders subsisted entirely on the basis of hunting and gathering. In some places the living was easy enough, through regular abundance of game, to support fairly fixed communities of these foraging folk. But there was as yet no hint of farming and no permanent settlement in long-lasting constructed villages, much less towns and cities. There was little social hierarchy, no specialised crafts like metalworking, no writing. Nonetheless, by about 13,000 years ago, human beings had spread across Siberia to the Americas, the final zone of global conquest to be achieved until Antarctica was fitfully brought into the human orbit in the last century.

It was environmental change after the close of the latest of the series of ice ages about 12,000 years ago that offered human cleverness, at different times and in different places, the opportunity to adapt to a new ecological niche – a man-made one this time in the shape of agriculture and stock-rearing with humanly selected improvements in plant and animal life to exploit. Permanently settled living close to fields and pastures, with a great increase of population, heralded new wonders in the human story. The Hellenistic wonder-mongers might not have been impressed with the early products of this new way of life, but we – who know what had gone on before for so long – are entitled to be. The dry-stone walls and towers of prehistoric Jericho, built around 10,000 years ago, represent for their time an engineering achievement that rivals the pyramids in theirs. The making of fired pottery and, later on, the smelting of metals were technological novelties developed by prehistoric farming peoples.

Settled life on the basis of farming, with food surpluses that called out for bureaucratic administration (with the aid of the invention of writing) under increasingly powerful chiefs and their associates and with social specialisations ranging from metalworking to priestcraft, eventually saw the rise in some places of city living with state institutions. As with the multiple developments of farming in different places at different times, civilisation itself arose in various centres at various times. Priority goes by maybe a few centuries to the Sumerians of Lower Mesopotamia, who had established cities with state buildings and written records by about 3300 BCE. The beginnings of the Egyptian civilisation date from about 3100 BCE. Over in the region of the Indus Valley, which Alexander was to reach more than two thousand years later, the Indus civilisation (with its still undeciphered pieces of writing) got under way in about 2600 BCE. Chinese civilisation and the beginnings of the world's longest-lasting script date from about 1900 BCE, as does the non-Greek civilisation of Crete whose system of writing is another one we cannot read as yet. In the Americas, where farming had been adopted here and there in central and south America since about 5000 BCE, Peru saw the complexification of village life on the basis of a mixed hunting and horticultural economy, with the building of large earth-on-rubble mounds that had adobe brick structures on their tops, looking down on open courts between the mounds. But all this without writing – which is one of the key features by which a way of life is qualified as constituting a civilisation.

It is doubtful whether the Hellenistic world would have regarded many of the products of these early civilisations as wonders. Most of their constructions were out of perishable materials that simply could not survive in a very impressive state into the second century BCE. The Ziggurats of Mesopotamia were of mud-brick manufacture, long decayed (though sometimes restored) in Hellenistic times. But they would surely have impressed in their heyday. So would the rambling, painted palaces of Crete, but a combination of natural disaster (volcanic eruption of nearby Thera) and enemies' arson (Greeks from the mainland) had long put paid to their magnificence. The Indus civilisation as revealed by modern archaeology, whilst capable of considerable feats of hydraulic engineering, seems to have been a rather peaceable and even egalitarian enterprise by the standards of the day, without impressive temples, tombs and palaces. The wooden structures of the Chinese were too far away (and also perhaps too homely) to impress themselves on Alexandrian scholarship. If they could have seen the mounds of Peru, the citizens of the Hellenistic world would certainly have been surprised and very likely impressed, but after all these were just rubble and earth constructions with no lasting grandeur – which, we recall, the Greeks and Romans accorded to the Colossus of Rhodes even when it lay broken off at the shins and smashed on the ground. (It is worth noting, too, that a good many wonderful products of far-away peoples were not just too remote to come to the attention of the Hellenistic world but in any case too late as well. The Brazen Palace of Anuradhapura in Ceylon, the Aztecs' great temple by Mexico City, many of the pyramids of the Americas, the Sacsahuaman fortress of Peru, and the temples of Angkor in Cambodia are among the wide world's wonderful sights that postdate the Hellenistic listings.

The only entry on the Hellenistic list of wonders that was owed to the early days of civilisation took the form of the great stone pyramids of Egypt, especially the group of three finest products in that line at Memphis by modern Cairo. True, they were in the orbit of the Hellenistic world and, very true, they were made of a practically imperishable material that had guaranteed their survival into Hellenistic times. But it must be fair to say that, if the compilers of the sights and wonders lists had been able to travel the whole wide world and review the productions of all the ages, they would still have put the Pyramids of Egypt high on their lists, as we would have to do with all we know. The Egyptians were not the first to build in stone – the towers of Jericho, the megalithic tombs of western Europe (from about 5000 BCE) and the rock-cut temples of Malta (about 3000 BCE) attest to that, though it's unlikely that the Graeco-Roman sensibility would have been very taken with these barbarous and unsophisticated works. But the Egyptians did it at the pyramids with a standardisation of cut masonry and on a staggering scale like no one else before or since. Small wonder that the Pyramids are the only thing on the lists of seven sights that we can still see today looking substantially as they did when the lists were first drawn up.

Ruins remain (and have been excavated) at Ephesus and Halicarnassus and the British Museum houses bits and pieces from these sites. Up to a point, but not to much effect, the foundations of the Pharos are still extant. Olympia has been

The Lighthouse of Alexandria

archaeologically excavated, but of the wonderful statue of Zeus (which was, in any case, carted off to Constantinople after the closure of the pagan temples) nothing at all survives. The precise site of the Colossus of Rhodes is a matter of speculation and its wreckage (in which form it spent most of its life) has long since disappeared. And, sad to have to relate, it must be doubted whether the other wonder ever existed at all, at least in the form in which it was imagined. Whatever the Hanging Gardens of Babylon may have been, they too are long vanished without very much at all that can be even suggested as a remnant of their location. In the nature of things, something as organic (and subject to organic decay) as an artificially raised up and watered paradise of trees and flowers can hardly have lasted very long.

The Pyramids and the Hanging Gardens were on the wonder lists because the former could not be left off anybody's list of sights and wonders ever, and the latter appealed for sheer luxurious and romantic perversity of endeavour (legend said a king built them for a foreign wife homesick for the verdant hilly land of her birth). But the rest of the standard wonders were really Greek concerns and all, including the strictly pre-Hellenistic Zeus statue and hardly Hellenistic Mausoleum, were well cut out to appeal to the Hellenistic cast of mind. The Colossus of Rhodes, in particular, consequently makes a good place to start in detail with our look at the Seven Wonders of the Ancient World.

COLOSSUS

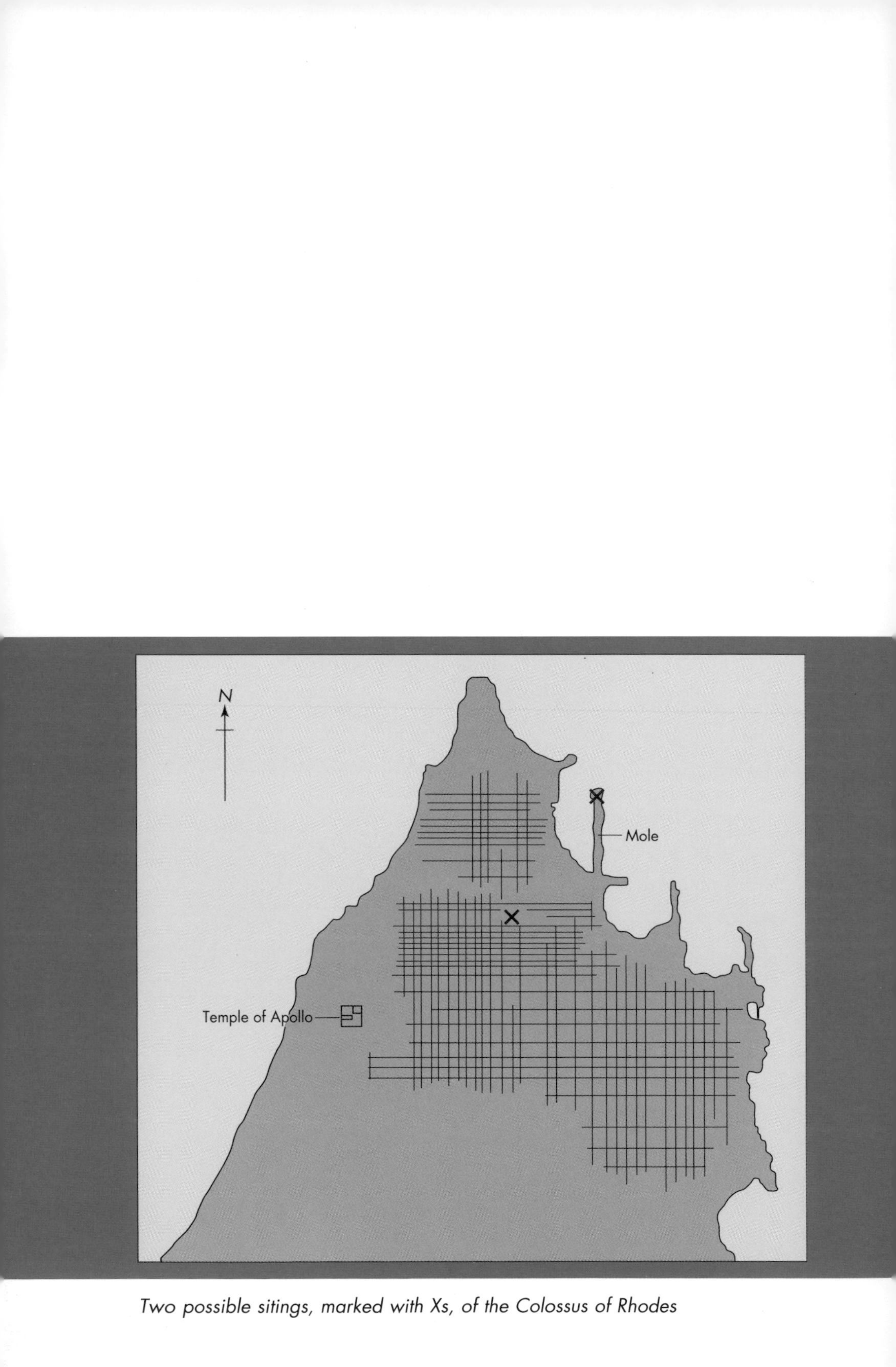

Two possible sitings, marked with Xs, of the Colossus of Rhodes

Chapter 2
COLOSSUS

THE island of Rhodes, 16 km off the south-western corner of the Anatolian mainland, sat on two ancient sea routes: between Egypt and Cyrenaica to the south and the Ionian trading towns along the Anatolian coast to its north; and between mainland Greece to the west and Cyprus and the Levant to the east. It was thus an island of the Ionian region of ancient Greece, off the Greek mainland and receptive of non-Greek influence from the interior of Asia Minor. Its relations with mainland Greece were therefore always likely to be ambiguous.

In 377 BCE it belonged to an Athenian-led confederacy, from which it withdrew at the urging of the Carian ruler Mausolus, whose huge tomb at Halicarnassus was, of course, one of our Wonders of the World. Again, in the course of Alexander's fight against the Persians, Rhodes sided with Persia against Greece under Alexander. When Alexander was clearly seen to be getting the better of the Persians, Rhodes went over to him. And when Alexander died in 323 BCE, Rhodes went with his general Ptolemy who based his power in Egypt rather than with Antigonus who inherited Macedonia, seemingly for commercial considerations.

The town of Rhodes in the north of the island had been founded in 409 BCE, from scratch when the island's three main cities pooled their resources. It was furnished with a grid layout of streets and a mole built out to sea to provide two harbours, one for the commercially all-important trade between Greece and the East and the other for shipbuilding and repairs. It is often assumed that the Colossus of Rhodes overlooked this second harbour.

Antigonus wanted this commercially vital island and its modern harbour city to desert Ptolemy and come over to him, and his son Demetrius (perhaps sarcastically dubbed Poliorcetes 'taker of cities') was sent to lay siege to the town when it would not. His nickname certainly went unjustified at Rhodes when, despite his possession of all the most up-to-date weaponry including a huge and sophisticated siege tower, Demetrius failed to reduce the town on his father's behalf in 304 BCE. The Rhodians emerged from their ordeal with a rather satisfactory arrangement: a freely entered into alliance with Antigonus under Demetrius that left them at liberty to pursue their commercial arrangements with Ptolemy, who had helped them against Demetrius and whom they called 'saviour'. In a manner not wholly characteristic of conflict in the Ancient World (or any since, for that matter) Antigonus and Demetrius seem to have borne the Rhodians no grudge for their defiance and along with other military gear let them keep the toppled siege engine. Perhaps it was not cost-effective to take that away: at all events, the Rhodians sold off the abandoned war materials and used the profit to construct a grateful memorial dedicated to their city's patron divinity, the sun-god Apollo under the name of Helios. The form this took was the gigantic statue we call the Colossus of Rhodes, and the commission to make it was given to a local boy, the sculptor Chares of Lindos. It was the astounding achievement of Chares in terms of size of bronze sculpture that gave the world the word 'colossus' in its familiar meaning. This pre-Greek word had previously been used of statues big and small: the Rhodian example fixed its use for bigness.

Head of Alexander, Archivi Alinari, Firenze

Chares was a pupil of the sculptor Lysippus who worked at Olympia and in Asia Minor, including Rhodes. He made many a portrait sculpture of Alexander from his patron's boyhood on and something of the Alexander look is likely to have got through into his pupil's realisation of Helios for Rhodes, as we shall see. The Colossus was probably made between the mid 290s BCE and 280 – Pliny says the earthquake that brought it down occurred some fifty or sixty years (copies differ) after its completion and we know there were earthquakes in 227 and 224 BCE. It took twelve years to construct, according to Pliny.

It is Pliny, Pliny the Elder to be exact, the Roman polymath who died in the eruption of Vesuvius in 79 CE, together with Strabo the geographer from Pontus by the Black Sea, who was slightly older than Pliny, to whom we owe what we most reliably know of the Colossus of Rhodes. The dubious Philo of Byzantium and a poem believed to constitute the dedicatory inscription of the statue add perhaps a little more information. The sources mostly agree that the bronze Colossus was about 33 m high ('70 cubits'), which makes it nearly 60 m shorter than the Statue of Liberty and about the same height (without Nelson) as Nelson's Column.

Pliny thought the Colossus wonder enough even in its overthrown state, with fingers larger than most everyday statues. And very interestingly from a technical point of view, he reports that its broken-open sections were seen to contain rocks inside that were employed to weight it, presumably to stabilise its otherwise perhaps rather flimsy structure. It is worth noting that Pliny had not seen the wreck of the Colossus for himself. He researched his *Natural History* as he tells us in his preface by reading 2000 volumes by 100 authors, whereby he garnered 20,000 facts about the world. It is calculated that, in fact, his fact count amounts to about 35,000 – among them his details concerning the Colossus of Rhodes.

Strabo thought the city and harbours of Rhodes were quite wonderful in their own right and was full of praise for Rhodes and the

The Colossus of Rhodes, as imagined by an early 20th century artist

Rhodians. He admired them for their naval prowess and seeing-off of piratical nuisances in the region – and for being friends of Rome, at the same time as long preserving their own independence. Their city, he says, was notably decked with votive commemorations of all sorts, especially in its Gymnasium and Dionysium. And then there was the Colossus: he adds the detail that the earthquake broke the figure off at the knees and no attempt was made to restore it, in accordance with a warning oracle.

From Philo, if we are happy to believe in his credentials, we learn that many mines contributed to the metal for the statue and that, in addition to Pliny's interior stones, there was an iron framework for the cast bronze exterior. Philo rated the interior complexity as more evident of laborious effort than the outside form. From him we might gather that the feet and ankles were cast first and everything else somehow cast on in situ, without prefabrication – this casting-on of new hot bronze onto cold bronze already cast is deemed impossible by modern commentators. They conclude that it must really have been a question of fitting plates of bronze to a stone-weighted iron armature: perhaps the plates were moulded onto this armature on the spot, but certainly not seamlessly cast onto any already set bronze outer surfaces. Philo does say that an earth mound was built around the statue and raised up with it as it grew, with the casting of next required sections carried out at the current top platform of the mound. (The siege tower of Demetrius would have come in handy for scaffolding.) He reports that 500 talents of bronze and 300 talents of iron went into its construction. If 500 talents represents about 13 tonnes of bronze, this quantity might seem to run to a rather thin outer skin for such a large statue, which might help explain the weighting with stones inside and the relatively large amount of iron used for the armature. (Incidentally, Philo's reasonable handling of these technical considerations in connection with the Colossus could be held to bolster the idea of a genuine core of material from the real second century BCE Philo of Byzantium buried in the rather fanciful general effect produced by some poseur of the fourth century CE. More fancifully, our Philo says of the work of Chares on his Helios that 'he gave a second sun to the world'.)

The idea that the Colossus stood legs apart across one of the harbour mouths of Rhodes is a medieval misapprehension, first retailed by an Italian visitor to Rhodes in 1395 who gleaned it from a local tradition which claimed the right foot once stood where the little round church of St John 'of the Colossus' was located in his time. For all its subsequent unshakeable popularity, the idea is a plain non-starter. The feet would have to have been planted hundreds of metres apart, which configuration is right out of scale with the known height of the monument, to say nothing of its total impracticality. In fact, to have had any chance of remaining standing at all, it is likely that the monument must have had a rather rigid pose in a solid, columnar form with legs close together. After all, an earthquake brought it down. And the also oft depicted pose with flaming torch raised on high is simply owed to that poem which probably records the dedicatory inscription of the statue: it sings of the Rhodians' setting up their statue and kindling the torch of freedom thereby – but it doesn't say the statue held the torch! A bas-relief from a Rhodian temple shows Helios in what looks like a saluting pose, shading his eyes with his right hand (from his own light, perhaps). It is possible that the Colossus was done in that same pose.

The fact is that we still don't know where the Colossus stood – the sources simply don't say. The (much later, as we saw) tradition that it stood across the harbour might reflect a dimmed memory that it stood somewhere by the harbour: certainly other, later statues belonging to Roman harbour towns like Ostia and Caesarea were set up at the water's side. It is possible that the medieval Fortress of St Nicholas (previously church of St Nicholas) marks the site of the Colossus. A circle of sandstone blocks in the fort's flooring may be all that remains of the statue's foundations, while some curved blocks of marble built into the fort's fabric (but too fine to have been cut for the purpose) may have come from the ancient monument's visible base, just as certain rough and oddly sized blocks lying by the mole may have originated in the interior of the Colossus.

This isn't much to go on and it seems a little unlikely to some modern commentators that the Rhodians would have left the extensive broken remnants of their great statue lying about to take up space by the side of one of their two harbours when the room could have been put to better use. But maybe the Colossus broken was just about as impressive in its way as the Colossus upstanding and the oracle against setting it up again may have contrarily conferred an extra special 'status' on it.

It remains entirely possible that the Colossus was not down at the harbours at all. Perhaps it stood in or by some temple of Helios that was built somewhat inland from those harbours, on higher ground so that the statue could still be remembered as overlooking them. Excavations conducted as far as the presence of the buildings of the modern town permit have turned up inscriptions that imply the existence of a temple up and away from the harbours, as well as masonry that seems to have belonged to it. The earthquakes are known to have demolished a good deal of the town at the same time as the statue and there is a report of the statue's fall as taking down houses with it. On the other hand, no traces of a base for the Colossus have been found up in the town and no furnaces, moulds, bronze pieces or clinker have turned up in the archaeological excavations. We just don't know where the Colossus of Rhodes stood, or how it stood, and we haven't – for reasons we shall come to at the end of this book – a single remaining piece of it. (Nor were any small-scale versions made of it, at least that have survived.)

But we do have a pretty good idea of what the head and face of the Colossus looked like. To go by a twice life-size head of the sun-god among the sculpture in the Rhodes museum, it probably carried a row of evenly spaced holes in the curls of its hair to hold bronze or silver spikes of flame, like the Statue of Liberty. Rhodian coins more or less contemporary with the Colossus show the sun-god radiating in that way. The face that Chares gave his Colossus sun-god would have been the one that his teacher Lysippus popularised in his renderings of his patron, the great Alexander himself. Lysippus, too, is known to have made some huge statues of the gods – a Zeus (at 20 m high) and a similarly gigantic Heracles. In his carvings of Alexander, Lysippus sought to convey an impression of character in a way that was new to sculpture at the time and he did it by novel means. The timeless formality of the classical style, the ideal made eternal, gave way to the realisation of the passing moment as a way of revealing character. To catch the fleeting moment in everlasting stone was at the same time a way of turning the momentary into the eternal: when character was revealed in the gesture of a moment, then character was just as surely realised for ever as the ideal was eternalised in classical sculpture. How far Lysippus truly caught the idiosyncracies of Alexander and how far he idealised him is, of course, hard to know: he almost certainly did both at the same time.

Something about Alexander's way of turning his head and tilting it up slightly, seeming to be looking far, far away, came home to Lysippus as both routinely characteristic of his patron and yet somehow suggestive of his extraordinary greatness too: human and more than a little god-like at one and the same time; and just exactly how Alexander wanted to see himself as his conquests and his taste for oriental sycophancy went more and more to his head. That turning, tilting, far-away-gazing head became the new image of semi-divine rulership on earth and a new image for the old gods, too. (It got through into early Christian art, for example in mosaics beneath the Vatican, as the first imagery of Christ the Light of the World, holding his head just so, radiating the light and fire of the rays of the sun, mounted in a chariot like old Apollo and Helios.)

The quite unclassical features of the man-god Alexander as envisioned by Lysippus are the features we may imagine Chares to have reproduced on the face of the Colossus at Rhodes, itself a vast expression of the spirit of Hellenism – which was to be seen at work on Rhodes as well as anywhere else in the Hellenistic world. For Rhodes, the largest of the Dodecanese islands and so well placed to trade with east and west, was an extraordinary commercial success in Hellenistic times, supplanting Athens as the leading maritime city of the Greek world (until it too declined when Roman power was being asserted in the east Mediterranean and Athens stole a march on Rhodes by turning Delos into a free port). The city of Rhodes, so recently established when the three old cities of Rhodes joined forces (Lindos was one of them, where Chares came from), was in Hellenistic days a huge place by the standards of the time and five times larger that it would be during the Middle Ages. It is reckoned that, at about 200,000 inhabitants, the Hellenistic island was home to three times as many people as it is today. It was, in the true spirit of Hellenism, a thoroughly cosmopolitan place, ambitious and hedonistic, too: it was said of the Rhodians that they ate as if they were soon going to die and built as if they would live for ever. The Colossus is the island's most famous piece of statuary, but all the towns were well endowed with public works and adornments, especially the city of Rhodes itself. In later days the famous Laocoon group (rediscovered in Rome by Michelangelo) and the Victory of Samothrace (now in the Louvre) were Rhodian productions. Lysippus himself made his Chariot of the Sun there.

The patronage of the sun-god was long credited on Rhodes: aptly, since it always was and remains a very sunny island. Its foundation myth held that Helios himself fell in love with the nymph Rhoda and their seven sons (seven again!) were the first inhabitants of the island. In fact, archaeology reveals a Cretan presence there in the early second millennium BCE, followed by a Mycenaean one as the first Greek-speakers reached the eastern islands. At the very end of the second millennium, Rhodes was

A modern interpretation of the Colossus by the architectural historian Mac Dowdy. The 4th century BCE coin showing the sun-god is from Rhodes, as is the fragment of bas-relief

settled by Dorian Greeks from the Greek mainland. Nymphs apart, it is not clear how Rhodes (Rhodos in Greek) came by its name: rhodon means rose and a link with the wild rock-rose has been suggested but not widely accepted. But the long association with the sun-god is sure. The satirical writer Lucian of Samosata in the second century CE called Rhodes 'lovely as the sun itself', without satirical intent.

The Colossus, which stood for only half a century or so (however amazing it remained in ruin), is apt to hog the limelight in ancient Rhodes. But there was much more magnificence to the place than just this overthrown giant, whether it lay by the harbours or a little further up into the town, which stretched a long way south and west of the harbour frontage. Especially in the western suburbs rising up to the old Acropolis, the original grid street plan, laid out by the town planner Hippodamus of Miletus after 409 BCE, is still sometimes in evidence. The old Acropolis stands on the unexpectedly named Mount Smith, from which an English admiral of that name surveyed Napoleon's fleet movements in 1802. Around the Acropolis there were temples of Zeus, Athena and Apollo, and a stadium and theatre that have been restored in modern times. A fine Hellenistic city, and an exceptionally prosperous one in its long heyday which went on culturally after the commercial decline of the mid second century BCE.

The earthquakes around 225 BCE ruined far more of the city than simply the Colossus, which was perhaps exceptionally vulnerable. The Hellenistic world came to the aid of the Rhodians in a powerful way, with all three of the successor states of Alexander's empire rallying round. The Macedonian kingdom which oversaw the Greek mainland, the Seleucid which now controlled much of Syria and the east, the Ptolemaic which ruled in Egypt and Palestine: all sent gifts both practical and magnificent. The Rhodians had been on good terms with the Ptolemies since the time of Alexander's death, when the first Ptolemy – one of Alexander's Macedonian generals – took over Egypt. In their hour of need after the earthquakes, Ptolemy III even offered to restore and re-erect the overthrown Colossus, but the Rhodians preferred to heed the oracle that warned them against setting it up again. And so, after a very short career in its intended form, the Colossus became a wonder for what it must have been rather more than for what it now was, however much the broken pieces might still impress and arouse curiosity as to the statue's method of construction. The short life of this archetypal product of Hellenistic culture in all its original glory, followed by its long reach down the ages after its overthrow, aptly mirrors the not very extended course of Hellenistic civilisation as a coherent and integrated way of life. Alexander's successors could not keep it up: the Macedonians couldn't keep the lid on the Greek city states, the Ptolemies rather went native in Egypt and the Seleucids took their cue from Alexander himself in surrendering to the joys of orientalisation. It was to be the Romans, stepping in like the original Macedonians before them, who would sort out the Hellenistic legacy. But in art, religion, philosophy, social behaviour and political thought, the Hellenistic outlook continued to exercise a powerful influence, especially on the eastern half of the Roman empire. In the end, the Roman emperors half-orientalised themselves in turn and imposed a half-oriental religion, centred on a man-god saviour in very Hellenistic fashion, on the whole empire.

The sun-god Colossus of Rhodes was pure Hellenism in its flashiness, its gigantism, its ambition, its advertisement of commercial success and even, though it was ostensibly a religious monument, in its aggrandisement of a particular human form. It could only have been eclipsed as a monument to Hellenism if the audacious plan that one of Alexander's architects once put to him had ever been carried out: Dinocrates suggested carving the entire Mount Athos into a giant statue with a whole city contained in its extended left hand! With notions like that in the Hellenistic air, we can see why the Seven Wonders had to be so huge, daring and showy to get onto the lists. What other wonders of the whole wide world that were going up in the last two or three centuries before the Common Era might have impressed the Hellenistic compilers of wonderful sights, if they had known about them?

It is highly doubtful that anything going on in north-west Europe would have been deemed to constitute a sight worth seeing or wonder of any sort for the Hellenistic outlook. The hill forts of the Celts were prodigious earthworks, which might have pleased the Hellenistic taste for large-scale interference with nature, but the result was too obvious and unsophisticated. Celtic art, while novel and intricate, was not on a scale to delight the Greeks and Romans (who, of course, did come to know something of it in time). The achievements of the early Germans beyond the Celts were not of a kind to be listed alongside the Seven Wonders. In Africa, we may admire the fine terracotta sculptures of the Nok kingdom that flourished in what is now Nigeria at about the same time as the Hellenistic wonders were being first written up, but they could never have been objects of more than curiosity to the Graeco-Roman world even if they had come to its attention.

In the aftermath of Alexander's exploits at the Indus, a great empire arose in northern India in the middle of the third century BCE under rulers the last of whom – Ashoka – became a Buddhist and even sent missionaries into the Hellenistic world to his west, in the old Persian empire. But, again, it seems unlikely that any of this Mauryan empire's productions – including the tall inscribed pillars of Ashoka, on which he promulgated his ethical precepts – would have qualified as Wonders of the World in Hellenistic eyes.

Further east in China a true wonder did come into being after the close of the Period of Warring States, when the Ch'in reunited China, in about 220 BCE. The emperor Shi Huang Di joined up an existing series of shorter lengths of walling on his long northern border to create a single barrier over 2400 km in length. (Actually, most of what we now see of the Great Wall of China was reconstructed in the fourteenth to seventeenth centuries of our own era.) This, the only man-made feature of our planet's surface (discounting the lights of some of our modern cities) that can be seen from space, surely counts as a wonder of the world and might very well have given those Hellenistic compilers pause for thought if they had proper report of it. It had most of what they required for a sight more than usually wonderful to see: certainly vast scale, boldness of concept and determination in the engineering department; it had perhaps little of the luxury of adornment that they favoured, but then neither had the Pyramids of Egypt. The so-called 'Terracotta Army' of the same emperor and the whole funerary complex around his 50 m high and 1400 m round burial mound at Xianyang might have impressed the Hellenistic world, too. Interestingly, this ruler's actual 'mausoleum' remains intact to this day, unlike any of the Seven Wonders, including the pyramids.

The very existence of the Americas would have seemed wonderful enough to the Hellenistic world. There was some speculation among them about the possible existence of other lands beyond the ocean that they believed to circle their known world of the Mediterranean with extensions north, south and east in the forms of northern Europe, Africa and Asia. It was rather like the way we speculate about life on possible planets circling other stars: they really had no more to go on than we do, relatively speaking. But if only they had known it, there were diverse worlds of human achievement, sometimes with quite a history behind them, all over the Americas. In North America, at about the time of the real Philo and of Antipater, earth mounds were going up in Ohio (one of them just over 20 m high) over wooden burial chambers and great earthworks of geometric or zoomorphic pattern were being constructed. The Great Serpent mound snakes its way for 217 m along a ridge. But Philo and Antipater would scarcely have been impressed with these productions.

But they might have sat up and taken notice if they could have seen what was happening in Meso-America. In the Oaxaca valley of Mexico, the city of Monte Alban had grown to house about 15,000 inhabitants by 200 BCE. The building of stone pyramids, with temples or palaces on top (unlike the much older pyramids of Egypt), was under way in Mexico, on the basis of an earlier tradition of mound building in rubble and earth that was not uncommon in the Americas, North and South as well as Central. The great age of Meso-American pyramid building was still to come, but a start had been made. None of the American pyramids, perhaps, could ever quite match the impact of the uncompromisingly plain hugeness of the Giza Pyramids of Memphis in Egypt, but I believe the Mexican pyramids would have passed all the Hellenistic tests for wonderfulness if accurate account of them could have reached Alexandria, though the sometimes rather bloody and invariably grotesque religious imagery of the New World would hardly have suited Hellenistic sensibilities. (On the other hand, those sensibilities could embrace the grotesque Diana of the Ephesians, as we shall see with the Temple of Artemis later on.)

In South America, the subterranean galleries of Chavin de Huantar, under the stone-built platform at the focus of that Andean city, might have impressed, with standing stones down below that showed off jaguars, serpents, eagles, caymans and some human features: the so-called 'Great Image' stands 4.5 m high. Again, this sort of iconography is unlikely to have recommended itself to Hellenistic connoisseurs in an age when a taste for the impressionistic, naturalistic rendering of fleeting moments of real human experience was to the fore. The spiders, monkeys, birds and geometric patterns of the Nazca Lines were first being laid out in about 200 BCE, near the southern coast of Peru, but this imagery too – however impressive the scale on which it was carried out (simply by removing stones from the desert's surface) – lay on the other side of a vast artistic and ideological gulf from Hellenism, as well as on the other side of the world. A world of which *our* Ancient World, to which it is time to return, knew nothing at all.

LIGHTHOUSE

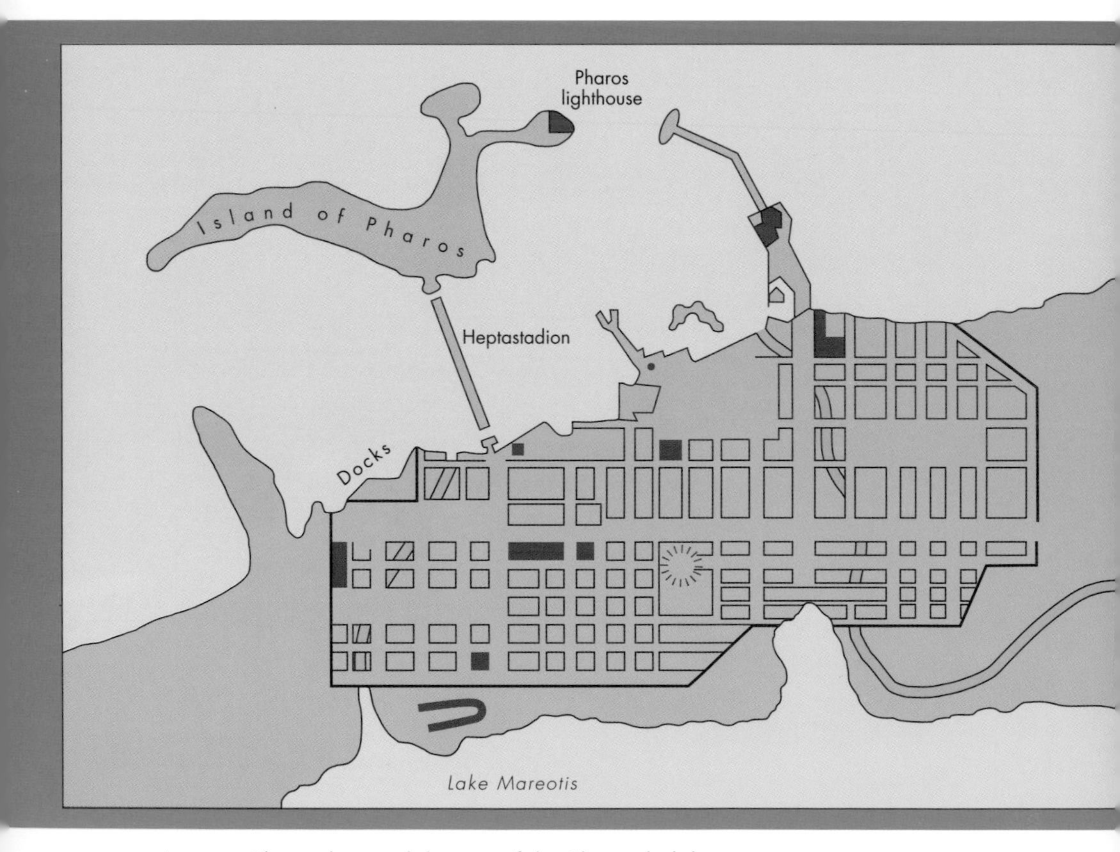

Ancient Alexandria and the site of the Pharos lighthouse

Chapter 3
LIGHTHOUSE

THE Pharos lighthouse of Alexandria was the last of the standard Seven Wonders to be established on the list. It was built at just about the same time as the Colossus of Rhodes in exactly the same cultural context of Hellenism, and right at the heart of the Hellenistic world, in Alexandria itself where the scholars of the Museum were gathering and sifting all the knowledge that was available to them.

The Pharos, a name – going back to the ancient Egyptian for Pharaoh's Island – which came to mean lighthouse in Greek (and in French and Italian, too), was called after the islet on which it was built, a limestone outcrop sticking up above the sand and mud just off the Alexandrian shoreline. When Alexander first passed by here on his way to the oracle at the Siwa Oasis, there was only a little fishing village where the greatest city of the Hellenistic world would be laid out. It was one of the many Alexandrias of the conqueror's empire (seventeen in all), but it was the brightest and the best, its layout designed – in slightly more sober mood – by the same Dinocrates who wanted to carve Mount Athos into a giant city-holding statue. Following the approach of Hippodamus who laid out the street plan of Rhodes city among others, Dinocrates created for Alexandria a very modern-looking grid with its main street running east to west. The limestone reefs and Pharos island to the west promised a harbour for the new city – hundreds of years before Alexander, the poet Homer was aware of this natural harbour.

The Delta shores of the Egyptian coast show little contour to guide sailors making for Egypt from Mediterranean ports. Nowhere in the commercial world of Hellenism were landmarks in shorter supply, and Alexandria was the hub of that world. It was perhaps as a simple daytime landmark that the Pharos 'lighthouse' was first conceived, without the light, of which there is no mention till Roman times: indeed there is no evidence of the systematic use of lighted beacons for navigational purposes in the Mediterranean until Roman times.

It is the familiar team of Graeco-Roman writers who tell us most of what we know about the Pharos directly from classical sources. Strabo says the Pharos island had on it, in his own day (the last part of the first century BCE), a tower of white stone with many storeys, named after the island. Strabo's contemporary Diodorus the Sicilian and Pliny the Roman of the first century CE also describe the Pharos and its situation.

A mole, extending from the city's strand out to the island, brought about two harbours, to east and west, one at least of which was always serviceable in any state of weather and sea: the Pharos overlooked the eastern of these harbours, guiding ships towards the port of Alexandria. (Lake Mareotis to the south of the city gave access to the Delta waterways and all the towns of Lower Egypt and to Upper Egypt along the single Nile stream south of Memphis.)

Construction of the Pharos seems to have begun after 300 BCE, during the reign of Ptolemy I, called 'Soter' (Saviour). It appears not necessarily to have been a state enterprise as such, directly ordered by Ptolemy and his consort Berenice. Strabo says the ded-

The little lighthouse at Abusir, along the coast from Alexandria. Photograph c/o John Ross (photographer)

icatory inscription on its base recorded that a friend of these sovereigns, one Sostratus of Cnidus (on a promontary of Asia Minor north of Rhodes), dedicated – and presumably funded – 'this monument to the Saviour Gods on behalf of all those who sail the sea'. Ptolemy Soter and Berenice were accorded divine status on coins issued during the reign of their successor, Ptolemy II Philadelphus who replaced his abdicating father in 285 BCE. Ptolemy Philadelphus sent an ambassador to Delos in the 270s of the name of Sostratus, so we might conclude that some early Ptolemaic bigwig who was a friend of the first Ptolemy and ambassador of his son was the driving force behind the erection of the Pharos. But Pliny, writing a little later than Strabo, says Ptolemy graciously allowed the architect Sostratus to put his name on the monument. This, of course, suggests that Sostratus was not the donor but the architect of the Pharos: rather a more illustrious role, perhaps, in our eyes but Pliny's remark only goes to show that the Ancient World would not usually have looked at it in that light.

According to Lucian of Samosata in the second century CE, an engineer called Sostratus of Cnidus helped the first Ptolemy, when he was still merely one of Alexander's generals, to capture Memphis by diverting the course of the Nile – in the 330s BCE, which makes it unlikely that the same man could have gone as ambassador to Delos some sixty years later. This sort of thing serves to illustrate how confused and confusing classical texts can be, written and copied by hand before the age of printing and still more before the modern age of scholarly referencing of sources. Perhaps there were two Ptolemaic luminaries named Sostratus, perhaps they were related, perhaps a later donor was mixed up with an earlier architect-engineer. At all events, it seems likely that if Ptolemy I had stumped up for the Pharos himself, the world would have known about it, via the inscriptions that survived on its base into Roman and even later times.

The 'Saviour Gods' of that inscription may not have been Ptolemy and Berenice at all, but rather Castor and Pollux who

A majestic rendering of the Pharos from the 1920s

Harold Oakley

became patron gods of navigation, or they may have been Zeus Soter and Proteus, the shape-changing old Man of the Sea whose home was often supposed to be on Pharos island. (This supposition was based on the chance correspondence of Greek 'Proteus' with the latter-day local Egyptian pronunciation of the island's name as something like 'Prouti', meaning island of 'perao', the Great House = our 'pharaoh'. Which may in turn give the reader a taste of the complexities of speculation about ancient mythological and philological matters.) We know that it was a statue of Zeus, king of the gods, that topped the Pharos in its original state, and the Arab geographer-historian al-Masudi of the tenth century CE says the eastern side of the Pharos carried, in full view of arrivals and departures at the harbours, an inscription in letters 50 cm wide dedicated to Zeus.

A combination of quite varied sorts of evidence, beyond the writings of Strabo and Pliny, makes it possible for us to know more about the Pharos than perhaps any of the other wonders except the still largely intact Pyramids: which is remarkable when we note that little or nothing is left of the structure itself and what remains is buried under a later construction or lying on the seabed, in the form of granite blocks from the load-bearing base of the monument. Much more survives of the fabric of the Mausoleum, but in pieces, and of the Temple of Ephesus, but in the form of archaeologically excavated materials. The Pharos, however, was pictorially represented in various media during its heyday and described in its latter days by Arab writers who went into rather more detail than the classical authors did.

From the Arab geographers and historians, we may garner evidence (if sometimes ambiguous) of the true size of the Pharos. Among Graeco-Roman writers, there was a tendency to inflate the dimensions of the structure and the reach of its visibility out to sea. Epiphanes, for example, made it out to be something like 560 m tall and Lucian claimed it could be seen from 300 miles away which, even if we allow for an ancient mile's shortfall of 142 yards from the English mile, is still a very long way at some

450 km. Josephus writing before Lucian, in the first century CE, restricted its visibility to a modest but still useful 300 stadia, more like 55 km. Abu Haggag al-Andalusi (from Malaga, as it happens) visited Alexandria in 1166 CE. He says that at that time it was possible to walk over the mole to reach the island, at one end of which the substantial remains of the Pharos could still be explored. He records that traces of the inscription seen by his forerunner al-Masudi a century-and-a-half before were visible on the seaward side of the monument.

The entrance into the square first stage of the Pharos was located at this time quite high up in one side and reached by an arched ramp. There were rooms within this first stage of the structure and a ramp rising around to the top, which apparently reached to about 58 m with a platform and parapet. From this platform rose the second stage of the Pharos in the form of an octagonal tower with a staircase inside that rose by another 28 m. From that point the Pharos continued upwards as a round tower for perhaps another 18 m. In Abu Haggag's day, there was a mosque on top of the whole Hellenistic structure, which by a happy chance is depicted in a mosaic in St Mark's in Venice of just about the same time – with a domed top. (It has been suggested that the dome-topped phase of the Pharos served as a model for the minarets of mosques thereafter: in Arabic, al-Manarah means both minaret and lighthouse.)

Abu Haggag says the whole thing (perhaps he means minus the mosque) stood about 97 m high, with a 9 m or so base beneath it all. If the Zeus statue originally on top was about 5 m high, then we arrive at a three-tiered tower (plus base) rising to some 115 m above sea level. (This height makes the Pharos the next tallest building of the ancient world, after the Giza pyramids.) Sarcophagi reliefs from Roman times in Alexandria show Isis Pharia (the old Egyptian goddess Hellenised and associated with a shrine on the Pharos island) holding a three-tiered building, sometimes with flames coming out of it (more of that later) or in association with ships. Later, Christian sarcophagi also show the lighthouse, as do mosaics from elsewhere in the Christian world of late antiquity which sometimes specify Alexandria as the scene in question and usually depict a three-tiered construction. A painted glass beaker fragment from Begram in Afghanistan (once in the Kabul Museum) showed a similar structure in brick with windows up the sides and a statue on top. Windows are featured in modelled representations of the Pharos found in Egypt, in the form of lamps, and must surely have been incorporated in the original to light the internal stairs of the structure.

Further depictions of the Pharos are to be found on Alexandrian coins of Roman times, from the imperial reigns of Domitian through to Commodus, covering a period of about a hundred years from the late first century to the late second century CE (and testifying to the iconographical impact of the Pharos on the Alexandrians' idea of themselves). These coins add further details to our picture of the Pharos in its prime, including Triton statues blowing conch horns on top of the first stage (though usually, it has to be admitted, the three-tiered Pharos is reduced to two on coins, probably to fit it into the narrow frame available). Several of the early examples have the Zeus statue on top and seem to show the entrance low down. This low entrance location as shown on the coinage persists through the reign of Trajan and into Hadrian's, but coins of Antoninus Pius show the entrance higher up, in keeping with Abu Haggag's account of about a thousand years later. It has to be remembered that any long-lasting structure of the ancient world, just like such a one today, will have gone through many repairs and changes during its career – the Pharos had been in use for over four centuries by the time of Antoninus.

Perhaps the biggest change the Pharos saw involved the nature of the source for any light that it emitted. It quite possibly started life as mainly a landmark in itself, all white shining stone (marble, or a local white limestone) seen from afar off to sea in daylight sailing hours. The Ancient World preferred to sail by day whenever possible. But the classical sources, writing in Roman times a couple of centuries or so after the building of the Pharos, agree on the provision of a huge fire in the monument reflected out to sea by mirrors. Some speak of donkeys taking fuel to the top, of unspecified character: wood was always in short supply in Egypt and it is hard to imagine a sufficient supply of dried dung either to feed a fire at the top; an oil-fed fire has been suggested.

We know of Roman-period lighthouses with fires to furnish the light and mirrors to reflect it, presumably of polished bronze. Pliny mentions such beacons at Ostia, port of Rome, and at Ravenna: a mosaic at Ostia shows its lighthouse belching flames from the top and a medallion of Commodus shows a three-tiered lighthouse in similar action. Conceivably such mirror-equipped lighthouses could function in daytime reflecting the sun and in fuel-short but sunny Egypt that may be just what the Pharos did before Roman alterations. Apparently it was employed in that way again in early medieval times, before the building of the mosque at the top in about 1000 CE. (It's hard to imagine the Roman lighthouse at Dover in England being of much use if it had relied on sunlight.)

The Pharos is not available for inspection any more, but it happens that about 50 km west from Alexandria at Abusir, the ancient town of Taposiris (first built soon after Alexandria itself), there is in miniature another lighthouse that very much follows the design of the Pharos as we divine it from the old writers and the coins and sarcophagi. This little lighthouse probably served as a coastal subsidiary to the great Pharos, on a line of such beacons stretching west to Cyrene that were constructed in the late first century BCE. It is about one-fifth of the size that we reckon the Pharos to have been but it shows the same three-tier construction with a square base, an octagonal central section and a cylindrical upper stage, with traces of stairs to reach the top where, in its time, no doubt a fire was lit. It seems to have been built over a tomb and there are other tombs around it.

In Alexandria, little remains of Graeco-Roman times: certainly not the tomb of Alexander himself which was once the focus of the city's very existence. It may be that it is long lost to coastal erosion. Alexander's body was craftily intercepted in Egypt by Ptolemy I on its way back from Babylon to Macedonia and subsequently installed in an ostentatious mausoleum in Alexandria to fix the city's pre-eminence in the world that Alexander had called into being. The body was first enclosed in a gold coffin like the pharaohs of old and then in a glass sarcophagus, according to Strabo, which may indicate a fine, thin and almost translucent production in alabaster, of the sort that an ancient Egyptian ruler like Seti I, for example, was buried in, nearly a thousand years before Alexander. Likewise long lost are the palaces with their magnificent gardens and the Museum which Strabo mentions and also the wonderful Library, which unaccountably – since he did so much work in it himself – he does not. The Library of Alexandria, by far the greatest in the Ancient World, was first accidentally damaged by fire during Caesar's operations against Pompey in 47 BCE, further depleted by devastation of the palace quarter in the 270s and then maliciously wrecked by Christians at the end of the fourth century CE. What were left of the book collections of Alexandria after all that were piously destroyed by the Moslem conquerors of 641 CE.

The losses to civilisation at the hands of these assorted religionists were immense and awful. Many an ancient author that we know only in excerpts might have come down to us complete, solving many a literary and historical problem and affording much pleasure. But the reach of Alexandrian scholarship was not altogether cut short. Alexandria was the place where the definitive texts of all sorts of ancient literature were established, to be sent around the

Mac Dowdy's modern reconstruction of the Pharos. The coin with a depiction of the lighthouse was minted in Alexandria at the time of the emperor Hadrian

world in copies that, copied again, have in some cases survived and form the basis of our knowledge of ancient literature and thought.

The scholars of the Museum, according to Strabo, were funded and boarded at the Ptolemaic state's expense and were not necessarily required to teach, only to research their fields with the best possible facilities of the time. Among them were mathematicians and scientists like Eratosthenes who calculated the circumference of the Earth (by measuring shadow lengths of fixed markers in Alexandria and way south in Aswan) to an impressive degree of accuracy – he also catalogued 675 stars. Euclid worked in the Museum, too, as did his fellow mathematician (also engineer) Archimedes, of the famous screw and other more military contraptions. For the achievements of the Alexandrians were not just theoretical and academic: they could be practical too. The screw principle for raising water in an inclined trough or tube is still in use. The lighthouse, with its mirrors and its beacon fire (whenever that was first installed) was itself a pioneering piece of Alexandrian engineering and technology, the inspiration behind the Romans' more systematic installation of lighthouse chains from the first century of the Common Era on till the end of their empire.

Alexandria saw a succession of engineer-inventors who devised some striking machines that, one feels, might have led on to greater things in slightly different circumstances. The son of a barber of the city started his career with a counterweighted adjustable mirror for his father's salon. This Ctesibius, who flourished around 270 BCE, went on to design (and to construct, as we have no reason to doubt) such wonders as a musically singing horn (activated by the outflow of wine) for a statue of the queen of Ptolemy II in the guise of the goddess Aphrodite. He also worked on force pumps, a water-clock (with rack-and-pinion gearing) and an organ that ingeniously balanced its air-pump against a reservoir of displaced water so that pressure of compressed air was maintained in the sound-producing pipes at a constant level despite the spasmodic operation of the pump.

The extensive writings of Ctesibius belong to that vast lost literature of the Ancient World, so we know him only from reports by his successors. The books of his pupil Philo ('of Byzantium' – the one whose later impersonator wrote up the Seven Wonders) have survived in much better shape. His inventions include a novelty item featuring a nest of fledglings under a mother bird and a snake that threatens them: the snake rose up menacingly on a float as water filled up the bowl beneath the whole ensemble, and the mother bird's wings flapped up in response as a higher float subsequently pushed up the bird, whose pivoted wings were anchored by a wire to the bottom of the bowl. This charming toy was not, however, typical of Philo's output, for he specialised in the military engineering of such weapons as catapults and crossbows. He appears also to have invented the gimbal which would subsequently prove so important to the mounting of the magnetic compass, but the Hellenistic world did not develop this crucial navigational aid.

In the late first century CE, Hero of Alexandria improved upon his predecessors with a range of inventions that ran from everyday practicalities like self-trimming oil lamps and a prototype theodolite to a windmill-cranked version of the air-and-water organ, automata for theatrical shows and a sort of 'steam engine' which was more in the nature of a hot air turbine, capable of rotating a disc carrying figurines. With this latter device, in particular, we glimpse the possibility of powered heavy machinery that might have transformed the Ancient World nearly two thousand years before the Industrial Revolution in Britain, and then Europe and North America, in the nineteenth century of our era. But the truth is that metalworking skills, including lathe work, that were essential to that revolution were not available in Roman times and the Ancient World's reliance on slavery for its manpower put no premium on the development of powered machinery for heavy work that gangs of human beings could be forced to carry out, with even more callousness than nineteenth-century factory owners showed to their workers.

It's fun to think what the Graeco-Roman world would have been like with steam railways to provide rapid communication and rapid movement of goods and troops. Who knows what it might all have led on to? At Sakkara, by Memphis to the south of Alexandria, a cache of finds dating back to the fourth or third century BCE included a small bird-like object with flat wings and a very aerodynamic-looking vertical tail fin that was, no doubt, a toy to be thrown like a paper dart but which might have served as a model for larger gliders. And from a wreck of the first century BCE off an island to the north-west of Crete comes a complex multi-gear instrument that has been very plausibly proposed as a calendrical computer, of a sophistication we had not previously suspected in ancient times. This 'Antikythera Device' reminds us again how close the Hellenistic and Roman world came to our modernity in so many ways. In all times and places, people can be clever, ingenious and inventive. Some ways of living set more store by these attributes than others. It was Hellenism that saw the first light of a way of life we can reasonably call modern like our own, if not in all respects. That light was to be dimmed and distorted by centuries of theocratic power in the Christian and Moslem successor states of the Roman empire, but it shone again in the Moslem scholars' revival of interest in Greek learning and in the Renaissance's rediscovery of the Greek and Roman achievement. The Pharos of Alexandria makes a fitting symbol of that light. With our next Wonder of the Ancient World, we shall be drawn back into earlier and perhaps less well-lighted times.

MAUSOLEUM

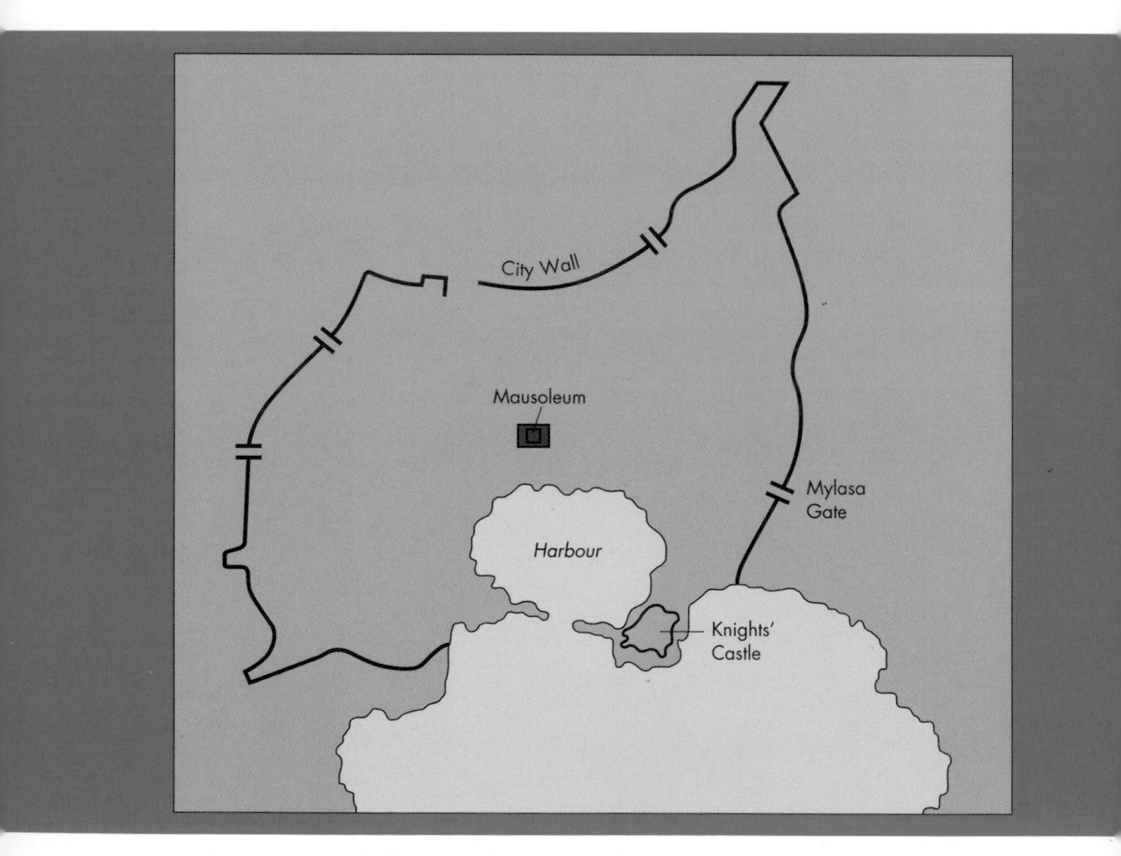

Halicarnassus with the sites of the Mausoleum and Knights' Castle

Chapter 4
MAUSOLEUM

THE finer cemeteries of the Western world, especially the ones that were developed in the nineteenth century, are full of tombs that take their name from one prodigious tomb of a minor ruler of a piece of Asia Minor in the fourth century BCE. His name was Mausolus and his great monument was erected in the city of Halicarnassus where, incidentally, the historian and traveller Herodotus was born just over a century before the Mausoleum was built. Halicarnassus is Bodrum today, on the Turkish mainland north of Rhodes, in that coastal zone of Asia Minor long within the orbit of Greek civilisation.

Mausolus was a Carian rather than a Greek, descended from an inland people of this south-west corner of Anatolia who spoke an Indo-European language related to Greek. Nominally, Caria belonged to the Persian empire and Mausolus was a satrap of the Persian king, but he took advantage of the Persians' troubles to join the Satraps' Revolt and carve himself an independent dynastic role. His political influence reached far along the coast of south-west Anatolia and his relatives ruled Caria until the time of Alexander. His own reign ran from 377 to 353 BCE.

During his rule, he made Halicarnassus his capital (from 370) building walls, gates, streets, harbours and a palace, all on the most up-to-date town planning lines, and filling the place with Carians from the hinterland. Doubtless for dynastic reasons, he married his sister Artemisia and she it was, according to some ancient writers, who erected the Mausoleum for him after his death – and, by implication, before her own of only two years later. It seems too short a building span for such an ambitious edifice, so perhaps the plans for it, at least, were well advanced before his death. There is some evidence for earlier burials on the site of his monument – work on the Mausoleum, for example, cut into the staircase of an earlier tomb. It is very likely that the famous Artemisia of the Persian Wars, celebrated by her relative Herodotus though she fought on the wrong side as far as Greeks were concerned, was buried here in the fifth century BCE.

Artemisia of the mid fourth century, following her brother-husband's project, wanted to create in his Mausoleum a great monument to the founder of a new age of Carian independence and empire. They succeeded very well: so vast and lavishly adorned was the Mausoleum that it became one of the Wonders of the Graeco-Roman world and the word came to mean any tomb with impressive superstructure. There is little left of this first and finest of all mausolea now, though some vivid sculpture survives including two statues that may represent Mausolus himself and his Artemisia. There are signs that tomb-robbers turned their attentions on the Mausoleum almost as soon as it was finished (in the same way as went on with Egyptian tombs, including the Pyramids): the entrance-blocking stone, still in place, shows cut marks to its top and front that appear to testify to an unsuccessful venture in robbery. In fact, the Mausoleum as a whole seems to have survived in reasonably good shape until the thirteenth century CE, after which earthquakes and then the Knights of St John made short work of the whole thing, as we shall see, reducing it to a state that only archaeology can investigate. It was stray reports from Western travellers in the region of architectural frag-

Sculpture from the Mausoleum now housed in the British Museum. The horse came from the chariot group at the very top of the monument

ments lying around at Bodrum that prompted excavation in the nineteenth century.

Again, it is the ancient writers, chiefly Pliny, that we have to rely on for a general idea of what this wonder looked like in its prime. It was the work of Greek architects and sculptors, and evidently wore a generally Greek air, as the recovered sculpture demonstrates, but it was packaged in a rather exotic form by classical Greek standards, in anticipation of Hellenistic eclecticism. It was, after all, made for a non-Greek dynasty, however Hellenised. Pliny relates that Scopas (whom we know also to have worked on another wonder, further up the coast at Ephesus), Bryaxis, Timotheus, Leochares and Pythius all contributed to the Mausoleum. Pythius was responsible for the four-horse chariot group that topped the monument, and the Roman architectural writer Vitruvius says he wrote an account of the Mausoleum. Vitruvius, writing a while before Pliny, offers no significant variations in his version of the Mausoleum from Pliny's – probably they were both relying on the lost work of Pythius. (Pliny and Vitruvius concur in calling the Mausoleum one of the seven wonders of the world, without spelling out the complete list.) It has been conjectured that Pythius was the overall designer of the building, as we know to have been the case with the temple of Athene at Priene, about 50 km south of Ephesus. His lost book evidently described both the temple at Priene and the tomb at Halicarnassus.

The town of Priene, extensively developed under Alexander after 334 BCE, had been relocated a short distance in the mid fourth century BCE and the Athene temple was well under way according to the plans of Pythius, before Alexander came to the town. Alexander succeeded at Priene in getting his name incorporated into the temple's dedicatory inscription, now in the British Museum, in a way that he did not – as we shall see later – at Ephesus. The temple was built to the Ionic order with its dimensions and proportions worked out very precisely in the foot measure of the time, the whole thing conceived with a high

An impression of the Mausoleum painted early in the last century

degree of mathematical regularity. It has been said of both this temple and of the Mausoleum that they were buildings characterised by a hitherto unprecedented degree of regularity. Remarkably, and unlike the tomb at Halicarnassus, the temple at Priene appears to have had no figured frieze around it.

The city of Priene, a little later than the Halicarnassus of Mausolus, was itself a remarkable realisation of Hellenistic tendencies. It descended by four terraces from an acropolis on a cliff top that could only be reached by a long winding rock-cut stairway. The creation of the town required the quarrying away of part of the cliff to make room for it, a typically bold piece of Hellenistic interference with nature to be contrasted with an earlier Greek desire to live with it. The view across the Maeander Valley was magnificent. The streets were laid out on the grid scheme and the town was furnished with council chamber, town hall, market place, offices, shops and a stoa portico displaying Ionic and Doric architectural features in fine Hellenistic mixture. All in all, about as close to recarving Mount Athos as was ever actually achieved. If earlier classical times had been characterised by sober civic pride and modestly expressed religious reverence, then the indulgence of the whims of rulers and the services of their propaganda are well expressed in places like Priene and, especially, Halicarnassus.

The artists themselves who created the temples for rulers to endow and the tombs for them to lie in were also beginning to feel their feet on the eve of Hellenism, where once they would have worked more modestly for the glory of the state and its old religion. According to Pliny (relying on Pythius?), the sculptural embellishment of the Mausoleum was not complete when Artemisia died, but the redoubtable team of sculptors carried on with their work to completion, as much for the sake of their reputations and as a monument to themselves as out of loyalty to their deceased patrons. When individual rulers started to employ artists for their own glorification, the artists were bound to make the most of their part in the outcome.

Pliny says the Mausoleum stood 140 feet (classical feet, of about 32 cm) high and 63 of these feet long, with shorter front and back façades. But, as he also says the four sides of the monument amounted to 440 feet, it is hard to see how the short sides can have been shorter than the long ones, and Pliny himself must have erred on the short side with the lengths of the long sides! Corner blocks still in place, and found by modern excavations, suggest 38 × 32 m as the actual base dimensions of the Mausoleum. Pliny's detailed figures for the height of the monument more or less add up to a coherent picture: the basal stage was about 12 m high, topped by a platform with thirty-six columns around it (parts of which have been found by excavation, with fine Ionic capitals) and platform and columns contributed another 12 m or so; the columns in turn supported a twenty-four-step pyramid, possibly of Egyptian inspiration, bringing the monument up by another 12 m, and the huge chariot group stood at the top of the pyramid. A fragment of chariot wheel has been discovered which, at over 2 m in diameter, indicates something like at least 6 m for the height of the chariot sculpture including a lost statue of the sun-god (more than likely bearing a close resemblance to Mausolus) at the reins. The architects must have had their anxious moments during the construction, getting the blocks of the pyramid up so high, to say nothing of putting some of the fine friezes and statuary up there, even with the aid of the cranes that were available by this time.

The massive pyramid would have appeared to passers-by to float in a truly wondrous way on the airy pillars of the middle stage of the Mausoleum, but in fact it was supported by the block of the inner core of the monument inside the colonnade (what would have been the 'cella' of a columned temple though here it was probably solid masonry) built up on the base section. The whole thing was composed for visual impact when seen from the ground

– hence the size of the chariot on top (and statuary on the higher levels) and the deep-cutting of the relief on the friezes that decorated various parts.

Pliny's descriptions and the archaeology on site illuminate each other, allowing us to picture the structure of the Mausoleum in more detail and in better general aspect than either line of evidence would allow on its own. Before archaeology began at Halicarnassus, it was noted that various pieces of what must be the Mausoleum lay around in Bodrum and had, moreover, in some cases been incorporated into the Knights' imposing Castle of St Peter there, looking down on the harbour. The Knights of St John had no regard for the 1800-year-old Mausoleum they knew, but even they selected a few choice slabs of frieze showing fighting Amazons, and sculptures of battling Lapiths and centaurs, to decorate their castle's walls, and they built in some lion statues that we know had come from high on the top of the colonnade, at the base of the pyramid. The Amazon frieze slabs were sent off to the British Museum by the British Ambassador in Istanbul in 1846, as were many more spectacular pieces discovered in the excavations that ensued between 1856 and 1858 under an assistant keeper from the British Museum. (Modern archaeological excavations at Halicarnassus were conducted by a Danish team from 1966 to 1977.)

An earthquake during the thirteenth century CE evidently brought down the upper part of the structure, casting materials beyond a 2 m high (or more) wall that once surrounded the whole monument. The lions from the base of the pyramid had been thrown far enough to fall outside this wall and a higher proportion of the largest statuary was similarly found beyond the wall than of the two smaller sizes (though all three are of greater than life sizes). This situation supports the surmise that, for perspective reasons, the statuary was graded from largest at the top through middle size among the pillars of the colonnade to smallest at the base. In all sixty-six statues or fragments thereof have been found, among them the big statues tentatively identified as Mausolus and

Artemisia. The 3 m tall Mausolus, if it be he, is an interesting piece of work, very 'Hellenistic' in concept, bulkily characterful rather than abstractly idealised and sporting a very unGreek moustache! This pair adorn the British Museum today, a long way from their previous perch among the columns of the middle section of the Mausoleum at Halicarnassus. Nineteenth-century excavation disclosed that some, at least, of the statuary had been coloured in its original state: a dun-red for flesh, brighter red for armour and drapery, with a blue background for the bas-reliefs. The lions were evidently, and naturally enough, painted yellow.

A recently discovered architrave block, reused as a lintel over a gate in the Knights' castle, has revealed the column spacing of the Mausoleum's high colonnade. Taken with Pliny's information about thirty-six columns, supposed to be arranged as eleven per side and nine per front and back with the corner columns counted twice, this spacing can be interpreted to mean that the platform at the top of the basal stage of the Mausoleum was narrowed to some 32 × 26 m from the 38 × 32 m that we know by excavation were the dimensions of the foundations of the base.

This matches a report that the Knights had discovered the base to widen as they dug down its sides – earthquake and decay had seen it part buried in soil formation. But we don't know whether there were any steps to this base's narrowing as it rose its original 12 m or so to the platform of the colonnade: we may presume so, to accommodate all the free-standing statues and other sculptures that have been found on site. It was an innovation of the Mausoleum's to have had so much sculpture attached to it, which it is hard now to assign to all its places on the building.

We do know archaeologically that the frieze of Amazons ran right round the top of the basal stage, immediately below the colonnade (there is a corner block of this frieze) and that the lions prowled around the base of the pyramid (blocks from the pyramid with the lions' emplacements have been found). If we assume that the smallest statuary came from the base, or a step near the base, of the monument and that the life-size scenes of battle were also close to the base, then we can assign the bigger sculptures of battle to a higher step, below the Amazon frieze. The large statuary, as we have seen, belonged among the Ionic columns of the middle stage. It remains hard, particularly in the light of Pliny's ambiguities (and the differences between different manuscripts of Pliny), to assign final proportions to the stages of the monument, which – together with the progress of archaeology on site – helps to explain the varying reconstructions of the Mausoleum offered by various historians and their artists.

What seems clear is that it was not so much the scale of the Mausoleum that earned it its place on the wonder lists as the truly spectacular character of its sculptural endowment, both as to quantity and quality: this really was a theama before it was a thauma, a sight before a wonder. There was, indeed, an awful lot of sculpture and statuary here, from the gigantic four-horse chariot on top to the life-size fighters at the base. And the statues were not done like the old representations of gods and men: these looked like real individuals, in the same way that the Hellenistic traditions would carry on.

The Mausoleum was mainly built with marble (brought in from elsewhere – for instance from the island of Cos and inland Phrygia), though with some blue limestone facing blocks and statue bases as well. Foundations were of a greenish volcanic stone. From the number of blocks reused by the Knights on site and recovered, and from the absence of any evidence of internal structure in the above-ground bulk of the monument, it looks as though the whole thing was solid from ground level upwards, with no rooms inside it. The underground tomb chamber of Mausolus was found by the Knights in the sixteenth century of our era and, apparently, only looted then (more of that at the end of this book): modern excavation has found fragments of his sar-

Mac Dowdy's up-to-date version of the Mausoleum. The statues of Mausolus and Artemisia, along with the lion and other pieces of sculpture from the monument, can be seen in the British Museum today

cophagus lid and stray spangles from his shroud. Butchered and burned animal bones found in profusion by the entrance to the tomb in the 1857 excavation remind us of the ceremonial sacrifices that would have marked the closure of the Mausoleum 2200 years before.

The Mausoleum, by comparison with the Greek temples of Asia Minor, looks to our eyes like a less than entirely Greek conception, however Greek its Ionic columns and its sculpture. The rest of it seems to have proceeded from several different inspirations. The pyramid suggests ancient Egypt as its model, though it may simply have been an architectural device to put a flashy great sculpture on top of the colonnade. The tall base beneath the colonnade may be related to the architectural tradition of Lycia to the east of Caria, from whose chief city of Xanthus comes the marble pillar monument now partly reconstructed in the British Museum. But it may equally have arisen from a desire to make the monument of Mausolus as unmissably high-rise as possible. This was the foundation monument of what was meant to be (and turned out to be) a long-lasting little empire of the ancient world: it was quite simply the biggest tomb of its world, after the pyramids. But it was not absolutely original: the Persians had been favouring lavish tombs for some time before Mausolus; and it may be that the long-vanished Theseum of the Athens Acropolis, of about 475 BCE, was a model for the Mausolus monument, intended as it was to memorialise the legendary unifier of disparate peoples into a new state – for Theseus, read Mausolus.

The Mausoleum may very well have given Alexander food for thought when he came to Halicarnassus in the course of his liberation of Greek Asia Minor from the Persians. It would have been less than two decades old when Alexander saw it, a dazzling monument to the founder of a cosmopolitan (Greek and Carian and all sorts) state carved out of the Persian empire. Alexander would go on to do the same on a vastly greater scale of ambition and achievement. The ancient world's grandest tomb (the

Pyramids of Egypt might be bigger, but they were nothing like as lavishly appointed) must surely have been in the mind of Ptolemy I when he appropriated Alexander's body and set it up in its gold, then 'glass' sarcophagus, in a magnificent tomb in the heart of Alexandria. Even so, it was the tomb of Mausolus and not the tomb of Alexander that was listed as a wonder of the ancient world and gave its name to a whole line of funeral monuments thereafter. Direct borrowing, incidentally, from the style of the Mausolus monument seems to have begun quite early: there are several much smaller-scale tombs built after it, of which the best preserved is at Mylasa in Caria (from where Mausolus had shifted his capital south and west to Halicarnassus); the Mylasa mausoleum still shows something of its step pyramid surviving on top of its twelve columns. A stroll around Highgate or West Norwood cemeteries in London shows how far the example of Mausolus and Artemisia would reach.

Just before the Mausoleum was built, a man named Herostratus set fire to a temple in Ephesus that was already about 200 years old. It was rebuilt to become another of the Seven Wonders, the one in fact that Antipater thought the most wonderful of all. The Temple of Artemis at Ephesus thus both shortly postdates and partly predates the Mausoleum. We will postpone our review of it for the sake of a look at a purely classical Greek temple – and the wonder inside it – that shows how far the Hellenistic world had travelled in spirit as well as in politics and commerce from the classical one. The Temple of Zeus at Olympia was built about a century before the Mausoleum and the statue of Zeus it housed a little less than that.

GOD

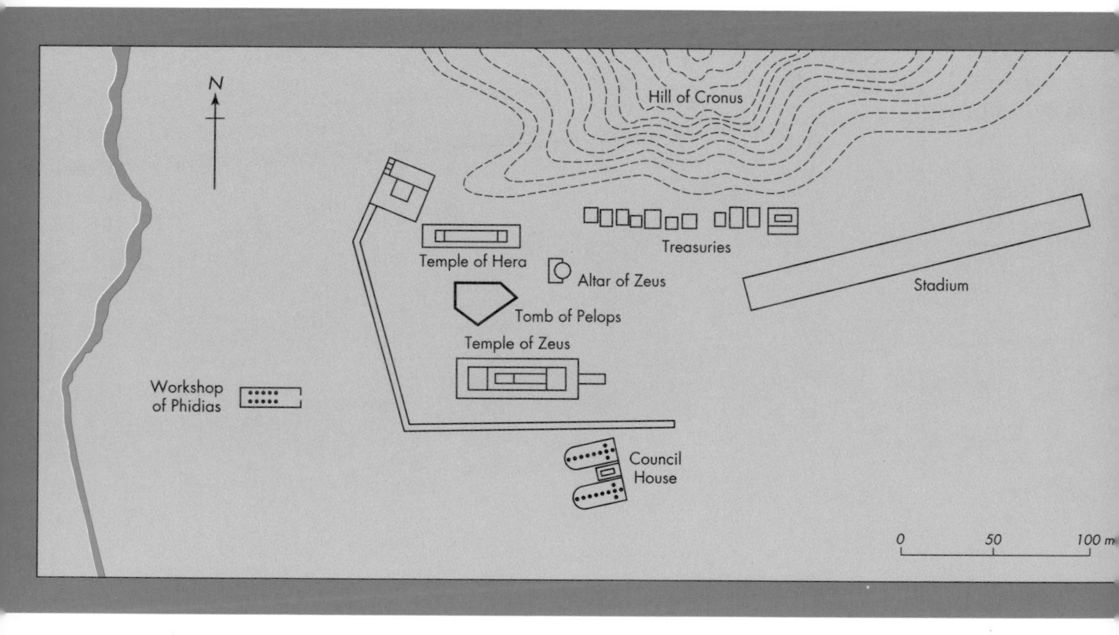

The setting of the temple that contained the Zeus statue at Olympia

Chapter 5
GOD

THE Wonder of Olympia resided not in the sporting facilities or the temples of this site of the original Olympic Games in a remote corner of the western Peloponnese, but in a huge statue that one of the temples contained. It was a statue of Zeus, king of the Greeks' Olympian pantheon of gods. (Mount Olympus, by the by, where these gods were supposed to live was far away in northern Greece.)

Most of the names of the Greek gods are already discernible in the Mycenaean world of the sixteenth to twelfth century BCE that is reflected in the epic poems attributed to Homer. (The *Iliad* and the *Odyssey* rest on oral traditions that go back to Mycenaean times, but the diverse material they contain was brought together – by one or more poets – at around 700 BCE, give or take half a century each way.) The Olympian gods of the classical Greeks – they had other, darker gods, too, who did not live on sunny Mount Olympus – were conceived in human form as both gods and goddesses and constituted a pantheon whose individuals are recognisable among the deities of other, related peoples like the Romans, the pagan Germans and the Hindus. The name of Zeus, in particular, is closely related to the names of all the chief sky-gods of the Indo-European language group. In the colourful mythology-theology of the Greeks, Zeus was the supremely powerful god of the sky, very much the chief of the gods and father-figure among them – though he was not the first god by any means, having deposed his own father Cronus in order to assume his role. The popular polytheism of many gods with chequered careers (and doubtful morals, by our standards) ran alongside both a more mystical strain of Greek religion exemplified in the Eleusinian Mysteries, and an entirely philosophical approach to Deity seen in the work of people like Plato. For Plato, God was a single principle that he might for literary and poetic purposes sometimes call Zeus and God of gods, but he was hardly the same character as the one who figured in all the divine escapades of Zeus's mythological life.

Whether conceived more as a philosophical principle or more as an all-too-human but divinely powerful sky-god, Zeus tended always towards an identification with the strong masculinity of bearded early middle age. This was how the Greeks liked to picture him, and to realise him in sculpture. (If clean-shaven Alexander served as a prototype for Christ the Light of the World among the early Christians, then Zeus furnished the iconography of God the Father and Christ the Ruler of the Universe.) When they came to create the greatest sculpture of Zeus in his temple at Olympia, it was as a mature male, powerfully built and bearded in his prime, that the Greeks wanted to see him done.

Olympia in the Peloponnese has been called Zeus's second home, away from the snowy cloud-capped abode of Mount Olympus some 280 km to the north. The Olympic Games, reputedly held at Olympia as early as 776 BCE, seem to have been developed out of the mortuary cult of a king of earlier times called Pelops, who remains a largely mythological figure though he may have been remotely based on some prehistoric ruler of the Peloponnese. The tomb of Pelops was always a central feature of the sacred complex of Olympia, but Pelops was rather eclipsed by the rise in import-

The god from the Bay of Artemisium,
The Art Archive/Archaeological Museum Athens/Dagli Orti

ance of Zeus at the site of the Olympic Games. A tradition grew up that the games had been established by Heracles, a son to Zeus, and the growing importance of the games encouraged the growth of the cult of Zeus at Olympia: the games, unlike today's, always retained a religious character.

Olympia was not really a town but rather a shrine with pilgrims' facilities and all the paraphernalia of temporary accommodation for the games. The oldest structures on the site, of wood and mud-brick, predate 776 BCE by a long way, which shows that, as usual, the historical temples (and the games) were developed on a much older cultic basis, centred in a wooded grove called the Altis at the confluence of two rivers. The major of those streams, the Alpheus, changed its course in the end and – together with other vicissitudes – put paid to the whole site of Olympia until archaeological investigation revealed its ruins. The site was overlooked by a conical hill said to belong to Cronus, father of Zeus.

As early as the end of the eighth century BCE, Olympia was a renowned holy place and was becoming rich on its pilgrimages and athletics. The great outdoor altar of Zeus grew into a prodigious pile of ashes from the sacrifices over centuries that were made there during the games: nothing of that remains. But the great temple of Zeus in which was housed the greatest of Zeus statues survives in magnificent ruins. It was built between 466 and 456 BCE, to the design of the architect Libon, in the same classical style of Doric severity as the Parthenon of Athens. What was inside it for the first twenty years or so of its life was not the famous statue we are about to describe, but some cult object (maybe an earlier statue) from an older shrine at Olympia, probably the temple of Hera, consort of Zeus.

When the authorities of Olympia wanted to improve upon the focus of the Zeus temple with a new and suitably impressive statue, they looked to Phidias of Athens, a painter turned sculptor in bronze who had made a great reputation for himself for his chryselephantine creation in the Athenian Parthenon: a huge

An early 20th century visualisation of the Zeus at Olympia

statue of Athene in gold and ivory, finished in 437 BCE. Phidias was close to the Athenian leader Pericles and suffered with his friend and patron when Pericles came under political attack in the 430s. It was said that Phidias had immodestly put portraits of himself and Pericles into the battle scenes on Athene's shield. He was accused of procuring women for Pericles at his building site. Formal charges were laid against him of embezzling gold intended for the statue, both a criminal and an impious act. The charges were rebutted by weighing the gold sections of the statuary, which had been fabricated for easy installation and removal. After this unpleasant business, Phidias either left voluntarily or was exiled from Athens and so became available for work elsewhere.

He was just the man they were looking for at Olympia. Probably in his fifties at this time, Phidias had a wealth of experience and great renown. As well as Athene inside the Parthenon, he had also designed (if not for the most part executed) the sculptures on the outside which are now available for inspection in the British Museum: the only place where we are fortunate enough still to be able to appreciate his style. He had also done another vast statue of Athene (10 m high) that stood outside on the Athenian

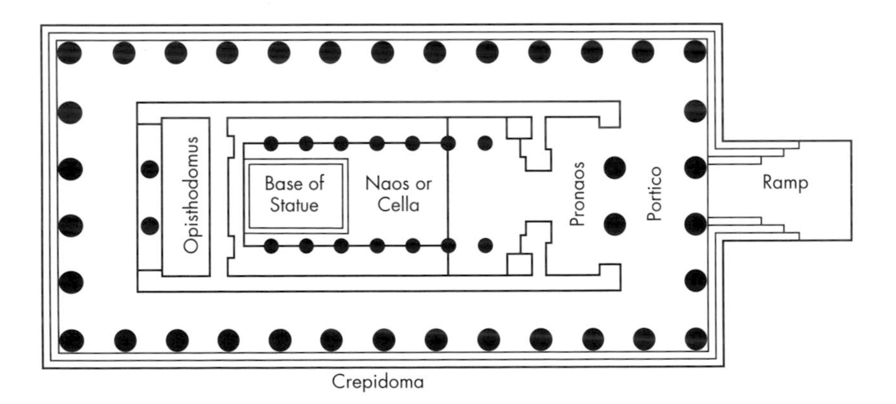

Plan of the Temple of Zeus

Acropolis, Athene Promachos ('the champion'), armed with a spear and a golden helmet that, when it caught the light, could be seen by sailors out at sea. Athene Promachos thus anticipated both the Colossus and the Pharos of the wonder lists.

Phidias with the Athene inside the Parthenon had devised a way of creating what looked like solid statuary on a grand scale out of ivory and metal plates fixed on an interior wooden armature. His standing Athene Parthenos was the height of a three-storey building and so was his Zeus – sitting down! Even in the seated position, the head of Zeus reached practically to the roof of the temple he inhabited and Strabo, who reported on Olympia as on so much else, thought the scale of the statue was rather overdone for the size of the temple, itself big enough, and left the viewer with the impression that the Zeus might stand up and smash through the roof above him. (A Roman ringstone in carnelian illustrates the up-to-the-rafters situation of the Zeus statue in its temple.) Cicero, however, slightly earlier than Strabo, credits Phidias with possessing a vision of such divine beauty that it was this quality that really gave the statue its impact. Philo aptly remarks that, while the other wonders were admired, the Zeus statue was venerated: its achievement made Phidias in one sense the father of Zeus. So we can work out what it was that got the Zeus statue onto the wonder lists: it was its intimation of divinity achieved through beauty and grandeur. Perhaps, additionally, it was its status as a realisation of Zeus, king of the gods, that gained it its place on the lists over the surely equally impressive statue of his daughter Athene. And perhaps, too, its aura of divinity over and above the usual portrayal of the gods, thanks to the achievement of Phidias at Olympia, deterred the making of copies of it on a small scale: as with the Colossus of Rhodes, there are no Hellenistic or Roman versions of it. There was, it seems, a large copy in a temple at Cyrene in Libya, but that is vanished too. The rather drawn-out and appalling fate of the Zeus at Olympia is a story we shall tell, along with the aftermaths of the other Seven Wonders, at the end of this book.

It is from written descriptions and from coins of the nearby city of Elis that we learn what we can of this most Greek of wonders. A poem by Callimachus, who came from Cyrene himself before going on to work so encyclopaedically in the Library of Alexandria in the early third century BCE, gives the measurements of the statue, which match well with archaeological investigation in the temple's ruins. The base of the statue was about 6.7 m wide and nearly 10 m long (remember, the statue was seated) and apparently over 1 m high, while the statue itself sat to a height of about 13 m. The much later Greek travel writer and geographer Pausanias, who flourished in the middle of the second century CE, contributes a very full description of the statue and its situation in his day.

Pausanias wastes little time on the temple itself beyond offering some measurements – about 70 m long, 28 m wide and about 20 m high to the pediment – and the interesting information that its roof was not covered with ceramic tiles but with Pentelic marble cut out as tiles. It was designed according to the rather plain Doric order and evidently built of a local stone of not very high quality which, after fire and flooding in later days, gives a rather dull look to the otherwise impressive ruins of the temple today. Pausanias was much more interested in what was inside the temple, which included more than the great statue itself, at least in his day. There were, among other things, bronze horses, a bronze tripod where in earlier times the wreaths of victors in the games were displayed and the twenty-five shields carried by armed runners in one of the races at Olympia. But, of course, it was the Zeus that Pausanias had really come to see. In the comparative gloom of the temple's cella, the entire statue and its throne were a riot of gold, ivory and precious jewels. Zeus wore a sculpted olive wreath on his head, as the victors in the games would do, and held a figure of Victory in his right hand. His left hand grasped a sceptre with an eagle perched on its top. He wore golden sandals and a golden robe, ornamented with animals and lilies. The throne he sat on was decorated with the full panoply of gold and precious stones, ivory and ebony. Pausanias really went to town on the throne, perhaps because he could see this lower part of the installation better than the figure towering above – and perhaps because it really was the most strikingly decorated part of it all. (Some reports suggest stairs and a gallery inside the temple by which a better view of the head could be obtained.)

According to Pausanias, each foot of the throne carried a figure of Victory in the form of a dancing woman and both front legs showed 'the Theban children seized by sphinxes'. This detail is supported by depictions on some local coins that show the armrests of the throne as the backs and wings of sphinxes and it has been suggested that Phidias took his inspiration for this motif from the thrones of the pharaohs in Egypt, which often featured sphinxes on their sides. Below the sphinxes, says Pausanias, Apollo and Artemis (we shall be coming next to her temple at Ephesus) are shown shooting down Niobe and her children – a reminder of the darker side of Greek mythology and religion which could cheerfully picture on the throne of the king of the gods the vindictive elimination of the children of a woman who had claimed that she was more fertile than these gods' own mother, the goddess Hera, consort of Zeus. (Roman copies of some of the reliefs on the throne attest to the violent imagery here, which included scenes of Heracles battling Amazons, and the stool that went with the throne was similarly decorated.)

The throne base is reported by Pausanias to have carried the inscription that 'the Athenian Phidias son of Charmides made me', while one of the struts of the throne showed a youth from Elis named Pantarces who won a wrestling match in the 86th Olympiad (436 BCE – just when Phidias was at work at Olympia). When Clement of Alexandria, a Christian writer of the late second century BCE, claims that the message 'Pantarces is beautiful' was engraved on a finger of the Zeus statue, we may perhaps be getting one of those odd insights into the everyday life of the past that always tickle us.

Under the throne and its stool, the marble base of the whole affair evidently carried more scenes from Greek mythology that showed gods and heroes and the sun and the moon. Pausanias says that it was impossible to get under the throne because wonderfully painted screens had been put up around it. He was writing in the second century CE, nearly 600 years after Phidias finished his work at Olympia. He says these screens, nonetheless, had been painted by the brother of Phidias (Strabo says nephew) and featured along with the Labours of Heracles some more of the darker sort of mythological imaginings of the Greeks: the story of Prometheus who stole fire from the gods for the benefit of mankind and was rewarded by Zeus with chaining to a rock to have his liver grow again every night so that it could be devoured again every day by an eagle. The sun-lit rationality of Greek philosophy went alongside a profound acquaintance with, one might say relish for, the cruelty in life.

The floor of the temple in front of the statue was, says Pausanias, paved in black stone, with some sort of rim of Parian marble around the black to form a shallow sump for olive oil. He says olive oil was good for the ivory of the statue (presumably poured over it from time to time) to prevent its deterioration in the damp atmosphere of the wooded grove in which the shrine complex at Olympia was situated. He adds that at Athens, the other great chryselephantine piece by Phidias – on account of the windy height of the Acropolis – needed water to stop its drying out.

Pausanias could see, looking up to the head of the statue well over 10 m above him, that on the highest part of the throne-back, above the head, Phidias had put the three Graces on one side and the three Seasons on the other, recalling that these six were named by the poets as daughters of Zeus. We cannot know exactly what the face looked like, for the coins are too sketchy to tell us much more than that it was, as we would expect, a bearded depiction of

Mac Dowdy's Zeus at Olympia. The coin comes from the nearby city of Elis

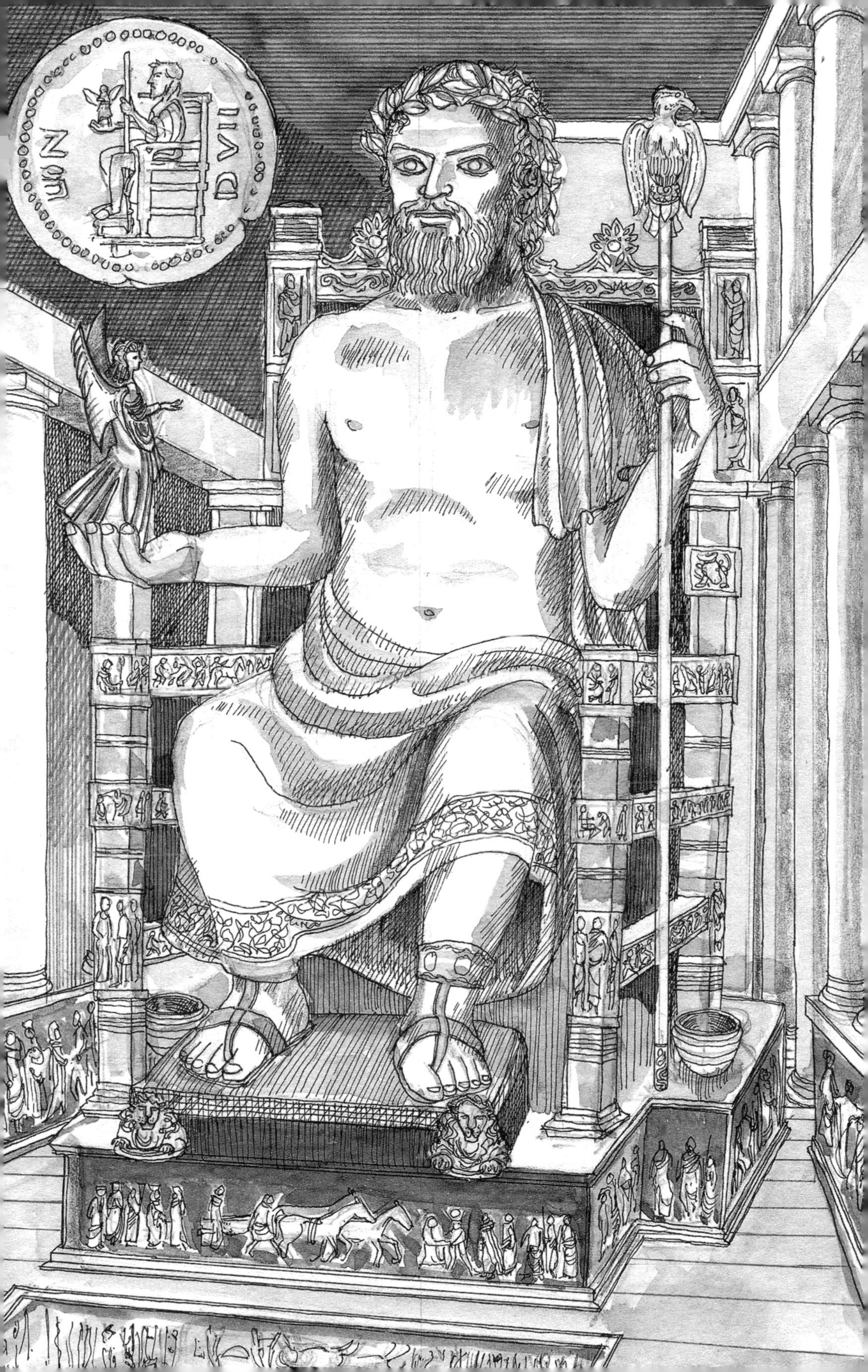

a god in his human prime. We can only hope that it was as good as the one some unknown sculptor put upon the head of a god (who might be Zeus or, perhaps more likely from the stance, the sea-god Poseidon) whose bronze statue fouled the nets of some fishermen from Skiathos in 1926. This powerful piece of sculpture now graces the National Museum in Athens and looks every inch the sort of god that Cicero says Phidias had realised with the Zeus at Olympia. By comparison with figures on well-dated painted vases of the time, this god from the Bay of Artemisium was made just a little before Phidias got to work at Olympia, in fact between 460 and 447 BCE. The Zeus or Poseidon from the seabed (from a wreck whose ports of call we do not know) is large but not overwhelmingly so: it achieves its effect by the sheer imaginative force of its concept and execution. Zeus at Olympia, on his throne with sphinxes, must have looked more like some huge statue of the Egyptians, pointing the way to the taste for the gigantic of Hellenistic times. When Plato wrote of the overweening grandiosity of the Atlanteans, it is hard not to think that he had partly in mind the enormous statuary that had come into fashion around the time he was born. What he would have made of the Mausoleum at Halicarnassus (built just after his death), which threw in as well as its overblown scale an orientalised hotchpotch of artistic traditions and the aggrandisement of a human individual's memory, we can well guess. It speaks volumes about the changes that came over the Greek outlook with Hellenism that Plato deplored this sort of thing and the Hellenistic world loved it.

A final detail of the description of the Zeus and its setting we have from Pausanias offers a fascinating insight into the ups and downs of political and cultural relations within Hellenism. In the temple of Zeus at Olympia, says Pausanias, there was a woollen curtain given as a dedication to the temple by Antiochus (IV, who had forcibly Hellenised Judaea and imposed the worship of Zeus on the Jews in 175 BCE). This curtain was decorated with Assyrian embroidery and dyed in Phoenician purple. We may conclude that it almost certainly came from the temple of Jerusalem where it veiled the Ark until Antiochus turned the place over to Zeus and had swine sacrificed to him there. In the Zeus temple at Olympia, the curtain could be raised and lowered on cords according to Pausanias, presumably behind the statue. It was not, then, a part of the Phidias design, but a novelty added more than 250 years later on.

During his visit towards the end of the second century CE, when that curtain had been hanging for nearly 350 years, Pausanias was also shown the very workshop in which Phidias had made the statue of Zeus. Some centuries after Pausanias, a Byzantine church was built on the foundations of the workshop about 30 m behind the temple, with dimensions closely resembling those of the Zeus temple's interior cella and on the same orientation as the temple, as archaeologists were quick to note. The workshop was even furnished with columns like the temple's. It seems that it was built to reproduce the size and lighting effects of the inner part of the temple for which its product was destined. Excavations around the church have revealed a pit for bronze casting and the rubbish of the workshop, including slag, earth pigments, lumps of modelling plaster, lots of worked bone and ivory and lead and bronze and iron, even obsidian (a black, glassy flint) together with discarded tools including spatulas and burins. There were spangles for the god's cloak, and terracotta moulds over which the gold of his drapery was hammered into shape: some of these moulds were numbered to show their place in the overall design. (Ivory, too, could be softened by boiling in vinegar or beer to prepare it for shaping, a technique used in furniture making before the time of Phidias.) In subsidiary workshop debris of the late fifth century BCE, a core of elephant's tusk probably indicates the need for ongoing repairs to the ivory of the statue, olive oil or no. There was also some rhino and buffalo horn among the debris: the chain of trade in the fifth century BCE reached far into Africa, via Egypt. The broken base of a fifth century jug found with the rubbish proclaims itself the property of Phidias, bringing us very close to the maker of the Zeus statue even as he worked on his masterpiece. Archaeologists don't estimate the floor of his workshop to have been substantial enough to bear the weight of the completed statue (so prefabrication of parts is envisaged there, for final assembly in the temple) but the walls of the workshop were heavy enough to guard the precious materials stored and worked on inside. As it happens, Phidias himself was accused at Olympia, as he had been at Athens, of misappropriation of materials, and the fate of this star sculptor of the ancient world was not a happy one, as we shall see.

Archaeologists have investigated much else beside the Zeus temple and the workshop of Phidias at Olympia. The stadium for the foot races has been excavated, revealing a square-ended structure unlike the later ones with rounded ends. The hippodrome for the chariot races has long since gone under the silt of the flooding Alpheus. Olympia has also disclosed to excavation a gymnasium and a once-covered practice track, an accommodation for VIPs and a suite of baths, but these are later than the time of Phidias. It is interesting to note that in the sixth century and fifth century BCE, the stadium offered open views towards the temples at Olympia, in keeping with the close link from early times of the games with religion. But Alexander's father Philip sponsored the building of a portico that closed off the temple view from the sports ground, just at the time when the games were 'turning professional' as we might say and losing their strong religious link, in the Hellenistic way. There are, by the by, inscriptions on statuary bases at Olympia that record that the statues were paid for out of the fines imposed on cheating athletes: the more things change, you might conclude, the more they stay the same.

With the statue of Zeus at Olympia, we have reached back to the fifth century BCE, to describe a wonder about a century-and-a-half older than the Pharos and Colossus, some eighty years older than the Mausoleum. The temple of Zeus is a little older still and the Olympic Games were reported by the Greeks themselves to go back to 776 BCE. The site of Olympia as some sort of cultic centre is plainly older than that. We are beginning to stray back into an older world than the world of the classical Greeks, as we shall again at Ephesus in the next chapter. What wonders of these reaches of time but on the global scale might the wonder-listers have considered for inclusion, if they had known about them?

If ample scale and a certain extravagance of décor were the more obvious criteria for inclusion on the lists, then probably not very much from around the world that dated to the centuries between, say, 400 and 800 BCE would have impressed the Hellenistic compilers sufficiently to be put on their lists. Things would not have been included just because, like Dr Johnson's women preachers and dogs walking on their hind legs, they had been done at all. So the nomad burials of the Altai Mountains beyond the steppes, of the same fifth century BCE in which the Zeus temple at Olympia was built, could only have looked like curious barbarian productions to the Greeks. At Urok, in the High Altai, a 25-year-old woman was buried, in a pit dug into the permanently frozen ground, dressed in what have turned out to be very well-preserved clothes of wool and felt and silk (from China or India) and tattooed like others of her tribe discovered in the barrows of Pazyryk. Vivid wall hangings, bridles and other horse equipment, whole wagons have come from the Altai graves. The Greeks would have been surprised to know that these people existed at all (or that the land they lived in existed either), though in fact they were distantly familiar with relatives of the Altai nomads who lived north and east of the Black Sea, where the Greeks established trading colonies from the sixth century BCE. The Scythians, as the Greeks knew these people, had migrated there from Central Asia in the eighth and seventh century BCE: they were in fact speakers of an Indo-European language, like the Greeks themselves. But to the Greeks they were absolute barbarians, in the sense that they uttered only incomprehensible words, like someone going 'Bub-bub-bub' to the Greek ear. Herodotus, the traveller-historian of the fifth century BCE (he died about 420) visited the Black Sea Scythians and wrote them up, as people living a barbarous way of life in a very cold place. South Russia and Ukraine are littered with the burial mounds of their elite warrior class, including their women and children, sometimes full of gold and silver as well as weapons, wagons and horse furnishings.

In the sixth century BCE, the Greeks were coming to know the western Mediterranean through their trading centres and colonies along the coasts of Italy, France and Spain. Though this experience brought them into contact with various peoples like the Etruscans and the Carthaginians, their architectural products were not of a kind to earn them a place on the Hellenistic lists of sights and wonders. Western and Central Europe north of the Mediterranean, despite the wealth generated in some places by trade with the Mediterranean world, threw up no tombs or temples with any chance of satisfying the Hellenistic criteria for Wonders of the World.

In China, the period of the Warring States began about fifty years before the Zeus statue was made, when power was consolidated in a few major (but contesting) states after a time of many small kingdoms. There were some large cities during the period of the Warring States: Linzi had a population of hundreds of thousands and Xiadu, as investigated by archaeology, was divided into zones with walls to separate the royal and governmental zone from the area of the city's common housing, workshops and markets. An idea of the lavish lifestyle of the aristocrats of this period is furnished by the fifth century BCE tomb of the Marquis of Yi in Hubei Province, with its gold, silks and jade alongside a multitude of weapons and chariot fittings. There was a carillon of bronze bells in the grave, too. But it's hardly the stuff of Wonders of the World.

In the Americas, the mound builders of the south-eastern region of North America, whom we have seen still at work in Hellenistic times, go back (building mounds in rather a small way) to about 750 BCE, around the time of the inception of the Olympic Games, at least according to tradition. In Meso-America, the Zapotec city of Monte Alban came into being at around 500 BCE as a single regional concentration to replace formerly dispersed centres. The Temple of the Dancers at Monte Alban, itself a large flat-topped mound, was flanked by over 150 slabs of stone on which were carved the figures of naked males in postures that have been interpreted as dancing or swimming. Very likely they represent the corpses of enemies killed by the first Zapotec rulers of Monte Alban, in line with a long iconographical tradition of Central America. Hieroglyphs and date notations associated with the figures are among the oldest pieces of writing in the Americas. Again we may surmise that the Greeks of the time and in Hellenistic times thereafter would hardly have been bowled over by Monte Alban of the Zapotecs, or caused to consider displacing anything from their list of wonders in order to make place for it.

In South America, the Chavin culture of the Andes (that we have already noted as a contemporary of Hellenism, in its later phases) goes back to at least 850 BCE, but again without monuments likely to have been listed as wonders by the Hellenistic compilers. Across the Pacific Ocean from the coast of Peru, the gradual settlement of that ocean's many islands saw, from the ninth century BCE, the construction of some very impressive burial enclosures at the island of Pohnpei, with platforms and tombs enclosed by massive outer walls of basalt. They, too, would not have made it onto any Hellenistic wonder list, save as items of extraordinary interest for their time and place (especially when we recall that the Graeco-Roman world had no idea at all that such a place existed). But they serve to remind us of the universality of human skills and capabilities in all situations of life, however various the expressions of these qualities; and that the human imagination has most often produced its most enduring monuments in the service of its ideological beliefs. The ruins of the great temple of Artemis at Ephesus, with its rather strange image of 'Diana of the Ephesians', stands on a site hallowed by belief since prehistoric times, from at least as long ago as Chavin and Pohnpei.

TEMPLE

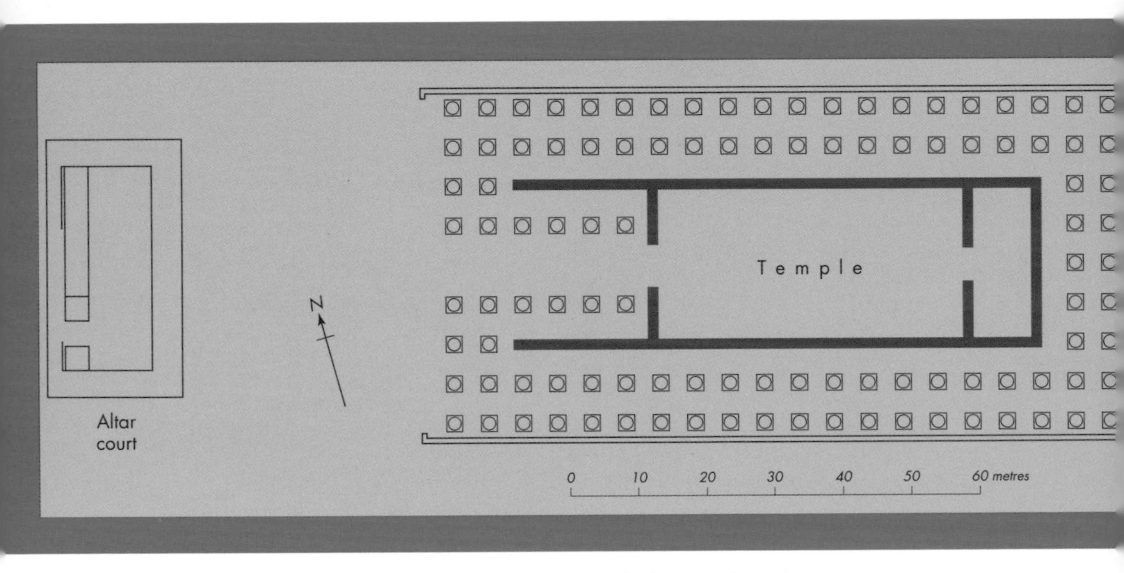

The Temple of Artemis at Ephesus, as revealed by archaeology

Chapter 6
TEMPLE

IT is worth recalling at the start that Antipater, the father of the wonder lists, thought the Temple of Artemis at Ephesus the most wonderful sight of all his Seven Wonders. Philo, real or bogus, went one better and claimed that anyone who looked on this temple would believe that the heavenly world of eternity had changed places with the earthly world. The temple Antipater knew was not so very old when he saw it (if we assume that he ever did, and wasn't taking literary liberties). It stood on the site of an earlier temple of the same basically Greek character, but it was itself a rebuild of the second half of the fourth century BCE. Rebuilding had been required because one Herostratus had deliberately fired the older temple in 356 BCE, on the day that Alexander was born it was said, for the sake of making his name famous. In this aim, Herostratus may be judged to have been modestly successful to this day.

Archaeology has revealed five phases of temple building on the site at Ephesus, with the burned-down temple's origins dating to about 600 BCE on the evidence of a coin collection piously incorporated into the foundations. Other finds from around the base of the temple's cult statue of Artemis include a miniature ivory sphinx and a large statuette of Artemis, stiffly posed but without the many breasts of later representations of this goddess at Ephesus.

Artemis was the Greek goddess we have already encountered on the throne of Zeus at Olympia, sister of Apollo. She was, for the Greeks, the goddess of wild animals and the hunt, and of chastity and childbirth. The Romans identified her with their own divine huntress Diana. She probably goes back to pre-Greek times on Crete and the Greek mainland: certainly she became syncretised with non-Greek deities when the Greeks spread to the coast of Anatolia, to produce the rather extraordinary many-breasted goddess celebrated in the temple at Ephesus. Homer called her 'Mistress of Animals' and it is her identification with wild, untamed nature – so often hostile to humankind – that helps to explain the pitiless wrath she often displayed, for example towards the children of Niobe on the Zeus throne by Phidias. In purely Greek iconography, she was frequently pictured with her quiver of arrows over her shoulder and her hunting dog or stag quarry.

This imagery is a far cry from the stiff, mummy-like figure (of ebony, gold, silver and black stone) that constituted the Artemis of Ephesus, as we know her from copies that survive of the original cult statue in the temple. Her garments there were decorated with reliefs of animals, to be sure, and also bees, while she wore a high-pillared head-dress on her head. The top part of her body was rather disturbingly festooned with a cluster of breasts that would have got in the way of the hunting Artemis. The theory that they were not breasts but eggs (or perhaps fruits) scarcely relieves the impression of biological freakishness the statues radiate. Eggs or breasts or fruits, the idea seems to be one of Artemis Ephesia as a mother-goddess, which the purely Greek Artemis never was. But Cybele, of the Phrygians (a people inland to the east and north of Ephesus) was such a mother-goddess. The Greeks usually identified her with their mother-of-the-gods Rhea, but it seems that at Ephesus the identification was between

A column base from the rebuilt temple at Ephesus, now in the British Museum, shows Hermes leading Alcestis from the underworld

Artemis and this not simply Phrygian but widely Anatolian 'Great Mother'. When the outraged silversmiths of Ephesus heckled the Christian propagandist Paul of Tarsus with cries of 'Great is Diana of the Ephesians', they were standing up for their old Anatolian Magna Mater, Artemis for the Greeks and Diana to the Romans, mother of men and beasts: and top-selling trinket on the local pilgrim market. We have seen, however, that a statuette from the foundation deposit of the temple, though rigid in pose, did not show the many breasts of the cult statue of the last temple at Ephesus. Xenophon, the mercenary and writer who died at about the same time as his friend Plato, says he saw in the older temple (to be burned half a century after his visit) a primitive wooden figure that we may think was perhaps the original cult object of the site, copied in the statuette from the foundation deposit. The original statue was supposed to have fallen down from heaven, to initiate the cult. A mass of jewellery, including glass and amber beads (some of them shaped like fruits) together with bracelets, buckles and gold rosettes, that was discovered by modern archaeology at Ephesus, might have decorated just such a wooden statue, Xenophon's 'xoanon'. We don't know how big that xoanon was or, indeed, how large was the later polymastic statue. Unless the story of the fall from heaven is only a conventional appendage, we might consider a notion of meteorite origin for the original cult object, in which case Xenophon's wooden item could have been only a stand-in. There is a story that a sculptor called Rhoecus fashioned the putative stone from heaven into the famous many-breasted statue of Artemis for the older of the Greek temples, in which case its absence from Xenophon's account is hard to explain.

But, unlike the situation at Olympia, it wasn't what was inside the temple at Ephesus that made it a wonder of the world: it was the temple itself. It was large and it was surpassingly beautiful. In its heyday, it was sited near to the sea, which perhaps even reached close to its altar enclosure, standing as a separate structure some way in front of it. The sea is now several kilometres away.

The temple at Ephesus, lavishly realised for a part-work magazine of the early 20th century

HAROLD
OAKLEY

Under the blue skies of the eastern Mediterranean, with the blue sea lapping up to it, the white marble temple at Ephesus must indeed have looked quite splendid, bigger than the Parthenon of Athens and lacking the Doric severity of the Zeus temple at Olympia. The Artemisium was done in the Ionic order (its columns topped with the characteristic round volutes) and with a certain amount of oriental exuberance, too. It was the largest completed temple in the Greek world, and among the earliest (in its pre-arson form) to be made entirely of stone.

The first Greeks we know to have visited this coastal piece of Asia Minor were Mycenaeans, before 1000 BCE. To the west of the Artemis temple, archaeologists have identified an ancient beach with a freshwater spring and a pathway leading to a small altar (and later Greeks left behind a layer of charcoal nearby that belonged to an altar of one of their early temples on the site). Mycenaean pottery has been found in this area, along with votive offerings of Egyptian, Phoenician, Palestinian, even central Asian origins, as well as from Anatolia and Greece, all testifying to the antiquity of the location as a cultic focus. No doubt the cult predates the Mycenaeans: the name of Ephesus may go back to the Hittites of Anatolia in the second millennium BCE, an Indo-European-speaking people whose word for 'bee' (always significant at Ephesus) was 'apusa'. There is, indeed, a Hittite record of the fourteenth century BCE that speaks of a fireball (meteorite?) striking down the king of 'Apashash'.

Ephesus seems to have been a colony of the Athenians, growing up in the late seventh century BCE. Two or three short-lived and wooden or mostly wooden temples preceded the first great marble temple whose foundation deposit coins indicate it to have been started between about 625 and 575 BCE. This temple is sometimes conveniently called the 'Croesus Temple' because the legendary – but historically real enough – King Croesus, of fabulous wealth, contributed greatly to the cost of its completion having spared the site in his conquest of the city (as did the Persian Xerxes later on). It is supposed to have taken a century to build, substantially from about 550 BCE, so Croesus cannot have seen much for his money here. He died in 546 BCE, having rashly lost his Anatolian kingdom of Lydia through an attack on the Persians as their power in the region was in the ascendant. Herodotus, born about 100 km to the south of Ephesus at Halicarnassus in 484 BCE, is our source for information about the Croesus funding of the first great temple at Ephesus. Interestingly, coins were first minted in the ancient world in Lydia in the late seventh century, with gold coinage from the mid sixth century. The use of coin money led to a veritable explosion of trade, from which the Greek cities of coastal Asia Minor profited particularly. (And not just financially: wealth from trade made for that independence of mind that is such a distinctive intellectual contribution of the Greeks, starting in the cities of Asia Minor, to world civilisation.) The coins of Ephesus often show the bee imagery associated with Artemis Ephesia and the priests of the temple there pioneered an early form of banking, using funds deposited in the temple's keeping to generate interest for their 'customers', with a commission going to the goddess (in the form of themselves).

Both the Croesus temple and the fourth century rebuild are known to us now – outside the pages of a few writers of Roman times – only as a result of archaeology. The Artemisium was, in fact, the first piece of wholly lost antiquity to be purposefully excavated for, in the mid nineteenth century of our era. From the Croesus temple there have been recovered, along with those foundation deposits already discussed, some fragments of statuary from around the bases of its columns. There are traces on these fragments of the 'Archaic Smile' that marks pre-classical Greek statuary of the sixth century BCE. With a century's building history, this first temple's construction and adornment run from the archaic forms of the sixth century into truly classical times. Pliny says four leading sculptors of the fifth century BCE, including Phidias of the Zeus statue at Olympia, vied to cast bronze sculptures of Amazons for the pediment of the old temple. (A story told of the Amazons' finding asylum in the temple of Artemis during their struggle with Heracles: they were supposed to have come from far away to the east and thus represent an oriental aspect of the Ephesus temple's décor.) Another archaeological find from this first marble temple, a drum section of one of its columns, carries an inscription to say that it was 'dedicated by Croesus'.

According to Pliny and Vitruvius, the chief architect of the old temple (his name was Chersiphron) used 'sand hydraulics', as we might call his method, to lower the lintels of his building onto the tops of its columns. The ancient Egyptians, with rather more sand to play with, used a similar system to funnel obelisks into position in their temples: carefully removing sand from specially constructed chutes to lower heavy things into position (of course, you had to get them up there first), with the added advantage of doing the work slowly enough to make adjustments – and take breaks – as you went. The story is related that, at the end of one working day, Chersiphron was too nervous to go ahead and get one particular lintel into position, even contemplating suicide to avoid the issue. But next morning, it was discovered that the goddess had done the job overnight, as she told him she would in a dream! Pliny also says that marshy ground was deliberately chosen for the site of the temple, as an anti-earthquake measure, with trodden-in charcoal and sheep's fleeces to stabilise the ground. Vitruvius reports that marble for the temple was discovered to be available about 13 km from its chosen place of erection and that wheeled cradles were used to transport the column drums and lintels to the building site.

The Croesus temple may have been roofed with wooden rafters and there may have been a wooden staircase to the roof. At all events, Herostratus was able to set fire to the place in the middle of the fourth century BCE, to sufficient effect as to require an entire rebuilding of the temple. Evidently the broad design of the original was followed, with the previous ground plan preserved in its dimensions of about 131 m in length and 79 m in width, but it looks as though the plinth on which the columns of the temple were erected was given nearly 3 m of extra height to try and solve the problem of flooding that went with the earthquake-proof marshy ground. The new temple was partly roofed over with tiles (which have been found by excavation) and equipped with water spouts, but perhaps it was partly open-roofed, too, over the statue of the goddess inside to give more light. The statue itself is long gone and so we don't know how tall it was, but Roman-period copies found outside in the courtyard were larger than life-size.

There were evidently three windows in the pediment at the top front of the temple, as some coins of the Roman period illustrate. One shows the central window (between the two flanking ones) with a gorgon face above it and the statue of the goddess between the columns below. Others show a female figure in the central window – in unmistakable continuity with an old Near Eastern iconographical tradition known as the 'Window of Appearances', whereby a god (usually a goddess) could be seen to reveal herself to her devotees. In the case of the Ephesus temple, the idea seems also to have been that the goddess within could look out and down at the walled open-air altar court some way in front of her temple where burnt offerings would be made to her. (Part of an ancient window frame used, like so much else from the Artemis temple, as building for later construction purposes in Ephesus may have come from one of the windows of the temple façade.)

Some coins show the four Amazons we know to have been commissioned for the (old) temple's pediment, presumably restored to their position in the rebuild or replaced. There were Amazons, too, among the sculptures of the altar court, where there was also another statue of the goddess. The wider courtyard around the altar was no doubt always home to a crowd of hawkers of religious trinkets, and assorted fortune-tellers and lower members of the priestcraft, selling off the less desirable cuts of the sacrificed animals from the altar (whose broken bones attest to the practice). They were all certainly there in Paul's time, and not keen to see their livelihoods threatened by an austere new cult. Ephesus, till the sea retreated, was a wealthy port: hence the hawkers, hence the bank.

Pliny says the fluted columns of the temple were some 20 m high, and numbered 127 in all, which is feasible in the light of modern archaeology but not proved by it so far. Pliny was recounting the situation of the final temple at Ephesus, but we have no reason to think the older, Croesus temple was different. The visual appearance of such a forest of columns was a new thing in Greek temple building in the sixth century BCE – Ephesus was the second place where it was done, after Samos. Probably the idea was inspired by travellers' accounts of the massed columns of the temples at Thebes in Upper Egypt. Some of the columns at Ephesus had highly sculpted bases and, it seems, Scopas whom we have already encountered at work on the Mausoleum at Halicarnassus was among the sculptors of the rebuilt temple of Artemis. A surviving basal column drum sent to the British Museum in the nineteenth century is interpreted to show Hermes leading Alcestis from the Underworld, in a finely composed and executed scene.

Rebuilding at Ephesus took place over a number of years after the arson of Herostratus. Alexander is said to have offered to pay for the finishing-off of the project if he could have his name upon it somewhere, as Croesus had done with one of the columns of the older temple. But he was very diplomatically talked out of this notion by the priestly authorities of the temple under their chief known as the Megabyzus, with the ingeniously flattering insinuation that it would not be proper for one deity to make offerings to another. It may, of course, be that the priests made this story up at a later date to aggrandise their establishment. Alexander's court painter, Apelles, is supposed to have done a picture for the temple showing Alexander seated like the Zeus of Olympia, so things must have been handled amicably enough if the story is true. (Alexander did succeed in getting his name on the Priene temple as we have seen.)

The temple of Artemis reconstructed by architectural historian Mac Dowdy, with a statue of the strangely endowed goddess

It was Alexander's policy to rebuild wherever he could what the Persians had destroyed during their wars with the Greeks. Of course, it wasn't the Persians who did the damage at Ephesus, but a Greek who torched the place in the year that Alexander was born. Fifty kilometres to the south of Ephesus, at Didyma, Alexander's policy saw the rebuilding of a temple of Apollo that in size and general appearance gives – even in its own ruined state (but not half as ruined as Ephesus) – a good idea of what the Artemis temple looked like. Indeed, it has been observed in modern times that the Didyma temple was every bit as deserving of a place in the wonder lists as any of the other entries, for its combining of scale and delicacy of execution.

Alexander was among the band of notorious characters who abused the asylum rules of sanctuaries like the Artemis temple. The mythical Amazons were reputed to have found shelter there from Heracles: rather more factually, the Persian king Xerxes sent his children to the temple after his defeat at the hands of the Greeks, to be taken under the wing of that first Artemisia (a relative of Herodotus) who had fought for him at Salamis and perhaps been buried on the site of the later Mausoleum at Halicarnassus. Alexander had two asylum-seekers taken out of the temple for execution. Three hundred years later, Mark Antony had Cleopatra's sister Arsinoe brought out and murdered so as to acquire the throne of Egypt for himself with Cleopatra, a descendant of one of Alexander's generals. More appealingly, the philosopher Heraclitus – a local boy – awarded himself asylum in the temple with the intention of getting away from the human race, understandable then as now. This thinker of the early fifth century BCE was the originator of the idea of the eternal flux, famously asserting – according to Plato – that one cannot step into the same river twice. The burned-down and rebuilt temple of Ephesus rather aptly illustrates his idea.

The rebuilt temple endured a long while, though. It was nearly 400 years old when Paul of Tarsus found it such uphill work to preach his Christian novelties in Ephesus. 'Diana of the Ephesians' had quite a long way to go in Paul's time, in fact another four centuries. And even when the triumphant Christians put an end to the cult of Artemis Ephesia, the local populace had only to transfer their affections to another rendering of the old Anatolian 'Great Mother' theme, in the shape of the Virgin Mary, who was now supposed to have lived at Ephesus in her later years in company with the author of the fourth gospel.

The long-sacred site of the Artemis temple at Ephesus has taken us back into the Archaic phase of Greek art and architecture and beyond that through the dark ages of Greek history into the time of the Mycenaeans, in the second half of the second millennium BCE. All this is a far cry from the Hellenistic world in which the lists of wonderful sights were conceived. In the second millennium BCE, the Greeks were not yet the top dogs of the eastern Mediterranean world they would become under Alexander. Coin money had not yet been devised. The simple alphabet that so facilitated commercial (and intellectual) communication in the Greek-speaking world of classical and Hellenistic times had not been invented (the Greeks would take their inspiration for that from the Phoenicians in the ninth century BCE, ultimately derived from the cumbersome and almost entirely non-alphabetic system of the Egyptians). The world of, say, 1600 BCE was a very different place in every way from the world of 200 BCE. The two remaining wonders we have still to contemplate belonged to the non-Greek world, one at about 600 BCE and the other of an immensely great antiquity. Before we come to them, let us see what the wider world could offer in the way of wonders and sights worth seeing back to about 1600 BCE, when the Mycenaeans came on the scene. It is worth noting, by the way, that the Hellenistic Greeks did not see fit to put any of their own ancestral Greek monuments on their wonder lists, though we know that they were familiar with the ruins of places like Mycenae itself. These things simply weren't grand and sophisticated enough to qualify as wonders, and we may be pretty sure that neither would have been most of the products of the wider world even if the Hellenistic listers had known about them.

Stonehenge, for example, which impresses us well enough for its prodigious achievement of engineering and its subtlety of astronomical alignments, hardly seems like the sort of thing the listers would have rated as a must-see wonder. It came to its final most elaborate form, though it was started very much earlier, in about 1600 BCE and some garbled report of it (as a very strange 'temple of Apollo') reached the Greeks and Romans, but its roughed out stones – for all the sophistication of the lintel locking arrangements – would have looked pretty barbarous to them. Much hard work and cleverness had clearly gone into putting it all up, but the Pyramids of Giza had all that in abundance and the finished products in Egypt were much more regular and monumentally overwhelming. It is true that the Pyramids were something quite alien to the Greek and especially Hellenistic Greek taste (in a way that the Babylonian Hanging Gardens, also entirely non-Greek, were not) and we may feel they were mainly listed for their immense antiquity and immensely ambitious construction, but we can hardly expect Stonehenge to have squeezed onto the lists on the same grounds.

Only the Pyramids in all Egypt made it onto the more or less canonical list of wonders (the Pharos being a Greek creation). There were plenty of other sights the listers might have considered, starting with the multi-columned (and, according to Homer, 'hundred-gated') edifices of Thebes in Upper Egypt and going on to the huge-scale carvings at Abu Simbel and the 'Colossi of Memnon' across the river from Thebes, among so many more from the second millennium BCE. But none of these wonders could oust the Greek entries on the standard listings.

Nor could anything Mesopotamian, beyond the fabled Gardens and the Walls of Babylon – though the great Ziggurat of Ur, for example, still stood in renovated splendour in the time of Herodotus, already 1500 years old, but never (at about 20 m) anything like as high as the Giza Pyramids. The wonderful palace of the defeated Persians at Persepolis, built in about 500 BCE, was burned down by Alexander in person when drunk: its scale and decorative richness might have made it worth an entry as a wonder, but it was never included, though the ruined Colossus of Rhodes was always there. This situation makes it unlikely that anything very much of what the rest of the world ever achieved would have been listed by the Greeks and Romans.

The palace complex of Knossos on Crete was, in its long heyday between about 1900 and 1400 BCE, a wonderful sight to behold, terraced on a hillside with a labyrinthine abundance of richly decorated (and well-plumbed) accommodations: probably one of the most attractive places in which to live and work ever created by the human race; but it was long gone in Hellenistic times. Away across the world in the Americas, the cult-centre at Chavin de Huantar in Peru, which we have already seen to persist into the last few centuries BCE, was started at about 900 BCE, while the gigantic heads of the Olmecs in Central America were being carved from about 1200 down to 600 BCE. These are all wonderful enough to us, and would no doubt have astounded the Greek and Roman list-mongers by reason of their very existence. But only two non-Greek and pre-Greek locations at Giza and Babylon featured on the wonder lists of our ancient world and the younger of the pair, in the form of the Hanging Gardens, is something of an odd-man-out that we come to next.

GARDENS

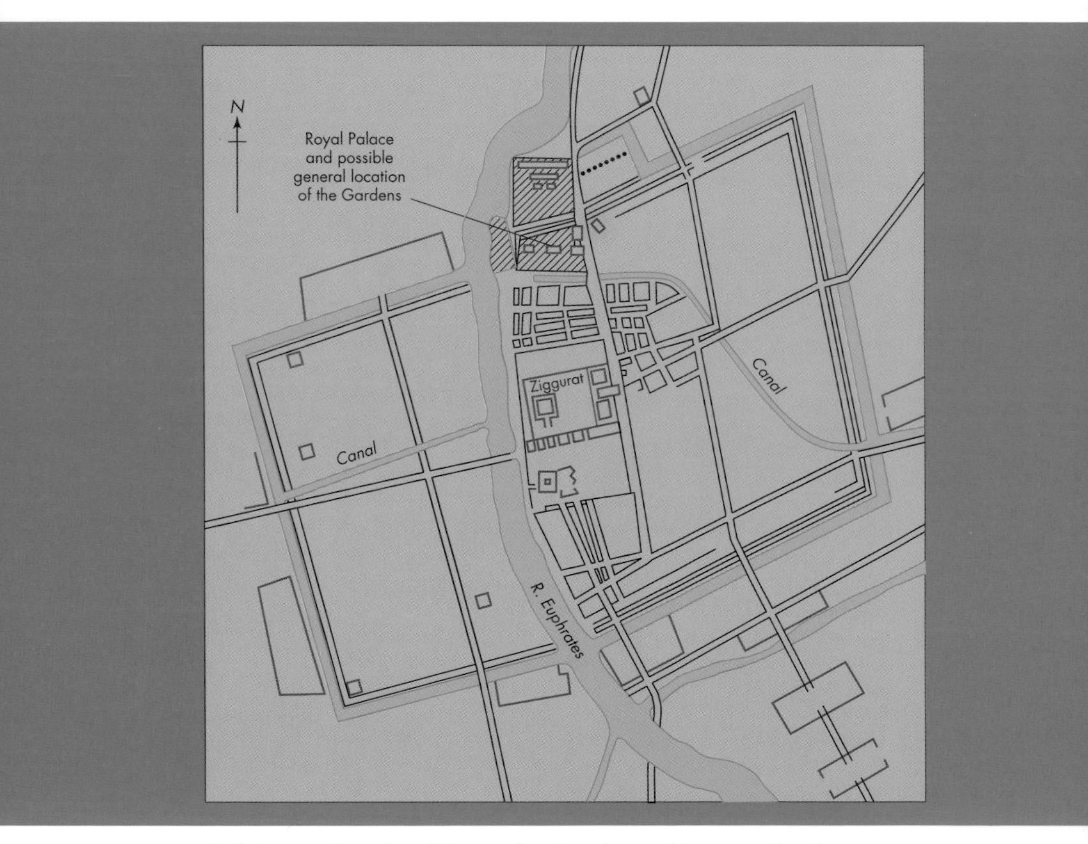

Babylon and a plausible site for the elusive Hanging Gardens

Chapter 7
GARDENS

THE Walls of Babylon, as well as its Hanging Gardens, were listed by Antipater and Philo as sights and wonders of their world. But the walls were eventually dropped in favour of the lighthouse of Alexandria when the list in the form we know was more or less fixed after the end of the Roman Empire. The Walls of Babylon were real enough and survive as an archaeological entity, but the Gardens are by comparison a matter of near-total obscurity. This gives them a rather different flavour from the other six Wonders, which were all rather compactly concrete items with, in four cases, something to show for themselves even to this day. The Pyramids of Giza are still there and clearly definable. The Temple of Artemis is well written-up and easily imaginable as a unitary construction – and we have found its remains. The Statue of Zeus at Olympia may have disappeared, but we have the ruins of the temple in which it sat and we can visualise its character on the basis of detailed descriptions and images on coins. We know where the Lighthouse of Alexandria stood and, again, coins and written accounts and comparable constructions allow us to picture it as a really existing thing. The

Colossus of Rhodes is wholly gone and we don't know exactly where it was erected, but its essential nature is clear to us from descriptions and easily apprehended as a single and distinctive creation.

The Walls of Babylon fall into the same general category as all the above – being clearly described, readily understandable as a concept and attested by archaeology. Our old friend Strabo (who lived in Rome from 29 BCE) evidently relied on some older Hellenistic source, or perhaps on the lost writings of someone actually in Alexander's entourage, in describing the walls as being about 10 m thick to their 20 m in height (with towers a little higher) and running a course of some 7 km round the city. They were built of compressed mud brick with straw reinforcement, baked for extra strength and laid with hot bitumen, at least in the case of the outer walls. A four-horse chariot (like the one on top of the Mausoleum) could turn on top of the wonderful walls of Babylon, according to Herodotus writing in the fifth century BCE, four centuries before Strabo. Excavations which began at Babylon in the last year of the nineteenth century of our era revealed a system of parallel walls around the city with an apparent infill of earth between them that might almost have provided a top surface on which four four-horse chariots could be driven abreast, as Philo asserts, exaggerating Herodotus. The walled city of Babylon was, moreover, the largest such enclosed habitation the world has ever seen: mainly the work of Nebuchadnezzar II in the early part of the sixth century BCE, in the wake of Assyrian destruction. He built its new outer walls and gates, renovated its temples, restored its canals, built the first stone bridge over the Euphrates and – or so he proclaimed – constructed its entire citadel complex, highly elaborate and lavishly decorated, in fifteen days.

Herodotus, describing the city of Babylon as it looked only a century and a half after Nebuchadnezzar's mighty efforts, mentions no Hanging Gardens. He mentions many things, including the (restored) ziggurat that overtopped the prodigious walls, but of

An Assyrian relief in the British Museum shows (top) a stylised garden scene with structures, trees and irrigation channels

any extraordinary gardens he says nothing. Perhaps we might make too much of that omission: after all, he doesn't mention the Great Sphinx at Giza either, being almost as much impressed there with the causeway leading up to Khufu's pyramid as with the three great pyramids themselves, in terms of the labour that had gone into it. Some people have speculated that the tiered ziggurat of Babylon, which Herodotus did appreciate, was the original of the Hanging Gardens, but in common with the other ziggurats of Mesopotamia it had no system of irrigation to bring the necessary water to it and no trees could ever have grown on its terraces. But it isn't just Herodotus who is silent about the gardens – they miss any mention in all the annals of Nebuchadnezzar and later Babylonian records. These accounts are, moreover, not at all sketchy but include building histories and even a sort of *A to Z* of Nebuchadnezzar's Babylon naming streets, gates and temples. The absence of the Hanging Gardens or anything like them is very striking.

First mention of them turns up in the work of Berossus of Cos, whose name and address might sound Greek enough but who was in fact a priest from Babylon named Bel-Usur and flourished around 290 BCE. (He is said to have settled on Cos, off the Anatolian coast by Halicarnassus, in later life, to found a school of astronomy.) He evidently wrote extensively in Greek to explain his Mesopotamian homeland and its history to the Greek world in Hellenistic times. His works have not survived in themselves but are excerpted at length in the writings of other authors, including Josephus of the first century CE. It has to be said that his accounts of Mesopotamian history have met with a fair degree of corroboration from Mesopotamian records discovered by archaeology. As retailed by Josephus, Berossus has Nebuchadnezzar creating for his palace stone terraces in imitation of mountains, planted with all sorts of trees to create gardens suspended in the air, as it were. A wife, it seems, called Amytis and hailing from the hill country of the Medes, longed for the scenery of her birthplace and was extravagantly indulged with the cre-

An impossibly romantic fantasy of the Hanging Gardens from the 1920s

ation of the Hanging Gardens. No Queen Amytis is attested in Babylonian records, but the general plausibility of Berossus means we should not rule out her existence or that of the gardens themselves, despite the silence of the Babylonian records and Herodotus on both counts.

Strabo, in the late first century BCE, talks of both Babylon's walls and its gardens as joint wonders of the world, siting the gardens on the bank of the Euphrates as it passed through the middle of the city. He says there was access to the levels of the gardens by stairways and water to irrigate them was raised from the river by very Archimedean-sounding screws, which arouses suspicion of anachronism and invention. Strabo's near contemporary Diodorus Siculus speaks of a slope of rising terraces resembling the seating of a theatre, about 20 m high. (Interestingly, while Diodorus attributes most of Nebuchadnezzar's building work at Babylon to an older and semi-mythologised queen Semiramis, he too favours the story of a later king wanting to please a homesick concubine as an explanation for the terraced gardens.) The terraces were apparently raised on vaulted supports, roofed with bitumened reeds over which two courses of mud-bricks were laid, with leading to retain moisture in the soil heaped on top of it all to a depth sufficient for tree roots. And pretty big trees they were, too, according to Curtius in the course of his *Life of Alexander*, written somewhere between the end of the first century BCE and the second century CE (with him, we just don't know): some of the trees were supposed to be 15 m high and over 3 m round, so that distant views gave an impression of a tree-clad hillside. That impression, if we are to take Curtius at face value, was evidently still available in the time of his sources, thought to be – as in the case of Diodorus and Strabo – people who had travelled with Alexander in the late fourth century BCE, including a sea-captain named Onesicritus. (Alexander died in Babylon in 323 BCE.) On the other hand, the Persian king Xerxes is known to have smashed up Babylon's walls and temples in exasperation at continuing opposition to Persian rule (which had rather peacefully incorporated Babylon under his ancestor Cyrus). It seems likely any fabulous gardens attached to Babylon's royal palaces would have suffered at the same time and not subsequently been available for inspection by Alexander and his entourage.

Diodorus recounts that the terraces of the gardens were watered by some sort of invisible machinery, presumably having in mind something like the screws mentioned in Strabo. Philo has the same idea, expressed in terms hardly consistent with his reputation as an accomplished engineer, which feeds the suspicion that the Philo of the Seven Wonders is a poseur of late antiquity pretending to be the real Philo of the second century BCE. He adds the notion of ploughing on the terraces of the gardens, with the whole thing supported on columns carrying palm trunks (capable of resisting damp) set close together.

Interestingly, he characterises the Hanging Gardens as a work of art produced by royal luxuriousness: in other words, as a high old extravagance of just the sort, we may conclude, that oriental fancy might create with oriental means at its disposal. One begins to suspect that the Hanging Gardens earned their place on the lists for being simply the most exotic *jeu d'esprit* apparently carried into concrete realisation that the Hellenistic world had ever heard of. But were the gardens so concrete in reality? We may think that, if Berossus and Diodorus and Strabo and even Curtius were capable of considerable accuracy about the rest of Babylon, then we may accept what they say about the gardens too, despite the silence of Herodotus and the Babylonian records. There is, unfortunately, also the silence of archaeology. It isn't quite total, but the fact remains that no direct archaeological evidence that can be seen to obviously belong to the wonder in question has ever been turned up – in the way that it has at Halicarnassus, Ephesus, even Olympia and Alexandria, to say nothing of Giza. Even the Colossus, though lacking direct evidence of its fabric or siting on Rhodes, is at least well attested in documentation (some of it still to be considered, when we come to the fates of the Seven Wonders).

The poetically-minded, as well as painstaking, first excavator of Babylon tried to believe that he had found archaeological evidence of the Hanging Gardens. Robert Koldewey thought that a feature of the Southern Palace (in the northern part of old Babylon) could perhaps be identified with the gardens of the Hellenistic and Roman-period writers. Fourteen vaulted rooms made up a subterranean crypt that might be thought to resemble the old writers' descriptions of strong arched or pillared supports for some above-ground feature attached to one of the city's royal palaces. There were three elaborately constructed wells in this crypt that might have supplied water – by some bucket chain arrangement – to facilities installed over them. Stone was used in this feature of the Southern Palace in a way that recalled the mention of stone in the terraces of the gardens by Berossus: it was otherwise vanishingly rare in brick-built Babylon. Koldewey thought perhaps stone was needed to support the weight of soil and trees of the gardens with some give in its foundations. He admitted that the identification posed many difficulties in detail, but thought it offered the best archaeological match of anything he found in his excavations at Babylon for the fabled Hanging Gardens. But it has turned out, according to written tablets found at this site, that the vaulted rooms were probably storerooms for rations, of oil and barley, to be spent on captive people held in the city, like the exiled Jews of the Bible. (Nebuchadnezzar was a great campaigner in Syria, Egypt, Palestine – the Jewish élite was carted off to Babylonian exile in 586 BCE.)

The Koldewey solution has the additional demerit of locating the gardens away from the river, in contradiction of the remarks of Strabo about its siting on the bank of the Euphrates (for what they are worth). In recent years, a site that really is on the river, to the north-west of Koldewey's vaults, has been proposed as a better possibility for the gardens, at a place where Nebuchadnezzar is known from his own claims to have built an extension to another of his palaces with a massive wall on the river. He does not, however, lay claim to creating gardens on this extension of any sort, let alone for a homesick wife called anything like Amytis. Deep drains have been discovered here, which might possibly have been associated with the run-off of irrigation, connected to another structure to the east that might possibly have been a reservoir, while further massive walls by the river in this same area might have been stepped in height as part of the terraced mountain-like scene-setting of the gardens. Unlike Koldewey's storerooms, the various features here have not yet been shown to be anything other than the terraced gardens they might be, but it is still only a matter of possibility and not the positive identification of the site of Babylon's Hanging Gardens, which increasingly come to look like some wilful Hellenistic misapprehension along romantic lines. Perhaps, starting with Herodotus and accelerated by Alexander's conquests and orientalising inclinations, it was the very exoticness of the whole great eastern city of Babylon, with its prodigious walls, that first brought on the idea of a listing among the Wonders of the World. And if perhaps a section of those walls on the river was indeed terraced and planted with trees for a garden, then maybe the idea of something very unusual in the horticultural line was itself planted in the minds of the armchair travellers who drew up the lists. In the end, the romantic idea of Hanging Gardens created for a beloved queen displaced the city walls as a wonder for people who were never going to actually see any of the wonders for themselves. If this be the case, then the gardens really are the odd-man-out of the wonder lists, lacking the everyday basis in factual existence in the full form ascribed to them that all the others retain. On this score, they align themselves more with, say, Solomon's Temple of the later Christian wonder lists, which also never existed in the state attributed to it. We may feel, too, that if the Hanging Gardens with all their fuzzy distance from reality, in the form they were supposed to take, could get onto the wonder lists of the Greeks and Romans, then so could half-a-dozen or so at least of the rival wonders from all the ages around the wide world that we have mentioned in this book.

That there should have been fairly marvellous gardens of some sort in Babylon is only to be expected. The idea of the paradise garden (paradise is a word from Persian introduced into Greek by Xenophon whom we encountered at the Artemisium) goes back to the earliest days of settled living between the Twin Rivers – Tigris and Euphrates – that feed into the head of the Persian Gulf. The earliest civilisation we know of, the non-Semitic-speaking Sumerians who predate the Semitic Babylonians and Assyrians of Mesopotamia, had reason to value the creation of irrigated artificial garden oases in their hot, dry corner of the world. Their successors all esteemed the idea of the garden: the Bible's Garden of Eden is part of the tradition.

For example, we know – from his record of it on a stela (standing stone) – that King Ashurnasipal II of Assyria in the early years of the ninth century BCE created an ambitious garden with canals and waterfalls at Nimrud, well north of Babylon on the Tigris, that was designed to remind him, in miniature – like the Emperor Hadrian's estate at Tivoli – of the diverse world he ruled over. At Nineveh, the Assyrian Sennacherib (who sacked Babylon in 702 BCE, a century before Nebuchadnezzar II was to start rebuilding it so gloriously) built himself a similar garden of exotica at Nineveh: a later garden there features in the Assyrian relief.

Of course, to maintain gardens in hot and dry places you need to lay on a water supply and it's rather convenient to let the water run down a series of terraces to do its revivifying work; close planting in the garden and high walls around it help to reduce the effects of warm and desiccating winds. Cyrus, who founded the Persian empire (and, incidentally, defeated Croesus of Lydia as well as freeing the exiled Jews in Babylon), made an elevated garden at Pasargadae in the foothills of the Zagros Mountains, where he was buried in 529 BCE. For this garden there is archaeological evidence in the form of the terraces themselves, with the remains of stone-lined watercourses, bridges and pavilions.

Believable but unavoidably conjectural, Mac Dowdy's Hanging Gardens are built on available archaeological evidence

So gardens there would have been in Nebuchadnezzar's Babylon and those possibly terraced walls with associated drains by the river may well have been one of them. Perhaps there was even a pining Amytis to make them for. It is doubtful whether the Archimedean screws, in particular, and the bitumen coatings and lead linings and rot-proof palm tree trunks and so on were necessarily parts of the scheme, but some methods of irrigation and water containment were certainly required. The 'high-tech' details of the Hellenistic and Roman writers sound anachronistic, and typical of their own technology, but who knows? As to what these so-called Hanging Gardens actually looked like, we can only conjecture. There is really less to go on than with any of the other Seven Wonders of the Ancient World: more artistic licence is required to conjure up a picture of them than with the Colossus of Rhodes, whose precise pose and actual location we do not know. The best we can do for now is assume some riverside setting with terraces and walls, plant it with trees and shrubs and have some water cascading down its levels – without going too closely into how the water gets to the top in the first place. It's a far cry from the grandiose (and impossible) reconstructions favoured in Victorian times or in the twenties of the last century. Indeed, pictured at this level, it's hard to see how the gardens could ever have been listed over and above a dozen or more other candidates for wonder status in the Hellenistic world. Perhaps, for once, the armchair sightseers and wonder-mongers were deceived by romantic hearsay about something they never saw or even, perhaps, never could have seen. That can certainly not be said about our next and final wonder from the listings of the ancient world.

TOMBS

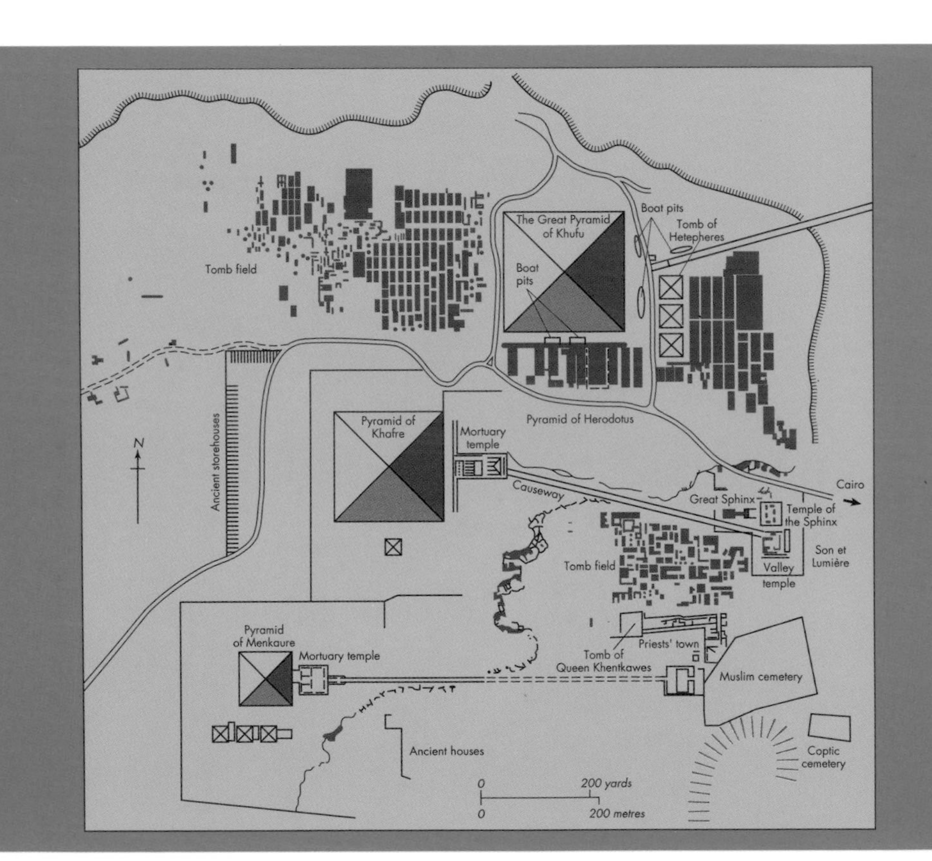

The complex layout of the Giza pyramids and associated monuments

Chapter 8
TOMBS

THE Croesus Temple of Ephesus and the elusive Hanging Gardens of Babylon took us back to a mere 600 BCE, only a few centuries in fact before the listing of the Seven Wonders began. With the Pyramids of Giza we face a great leap back into much earlier times – and into an even more alien world, if only the Greeks and Romans could have fully appreciated it, than the one in which Nebuchadnezzar flourished. Alexandria in the second century BCE was a thoroughly Greek city, with a Greek-speaking population and bureaucracy, ruled over by a Greek-descended dynasty – however much those rulers might from time to time put on the pretensions of the old pharaohs of Egypt. A Greek (and later on a Roman, too) might travel all over Egypt south of Alexandria meeting fellow Greek-speakers, including bilingual native Egyptians, everywhere he went. Of course, the lower orders spoke mainly or only their own Egyptian language, which survived alongside Greek (and much later on alongside Arabic, too, to persist to this day as part of the liturgical language of the Coptic Christians).

Greek contacts with ancient Egypt went back some centuries in

Hellenistic times and there were Egyptians fluent in Greek to educate the Greek world about their native history and culture – notably Manetho, a priest from the Delta region of the earlier half of the third century BCE, the time of the first two Ptolemies. Our scheme of Egyptian dynasties is still based on Manetho's writings. The Greeks were always a little in awe of Egypt's obvious antiquity – indeed, they were inclined to exaggerate it somewhat, so that Plato could write of 10,000 years of Egyptian history and have his character rub home the message by emphasising that, yes, he means literally 10,000 years. (Plato also professed to admire what he took to be the reactionary conservatism of Egyptian civilisation.)

Several lines of evidence, derived from the writings of people like Manetho and ancient Egyptian official records, from archaeological discoveries, from radiocarbon dating and from astronomical data, lead us nowadays to conclude that ancient Egyptian civilisation really got under way, with centralised government and written record-keeping, in about 3000 BCE. The monumental use of stone in tomb building developed during the first three dynasties to the point where, at about 2600 BCE, the first pyramid of Egypt was designed by the architect Imhotep for the Dynasty III king called Djoser. It was a stepped affair which went through several stages of enlargement during its building and was clearly based on a gradual elaboration (seen elsewhere at Sakkara) of an earlier style of platform-like tomb building, which persisted for lesser folk than the kings themselves. Though nothing like as large as the pyramids at Giza to the north of Sakkara where it stands, the Step Pyramid is a most impressive building, and all the more so for its associated features including outbuildings and enclosing walls.

But, justly, it has always been the Giza group, close to the old city of Memphis, and what we call the Great Pyramid of Giza that take pride of place among the pyramids of Egypt. Philo speaks of the Memphis pyramids and Strabo means the Giza group when he says three of Egypt's pyramids were really noteworthy – and

This model shows the smallest of the Big-Three Giza pyramids under construction by one of the suggested service-ramp methods.
The Museum of Science, Boston

two of the three, he adds, were among the Seven Wonders of the World. As a matter of fact, the second of the Giza pyramids, belonging to a king called Khafre (or Chephren in Greek), is almost as large as the Great Pyramid of Khufu (Cheops) but never arouses quite the same intense interest despite its associated temples and Sphinx, possibly because its interior structure has few of the mind-boggling complexities of its predecessor: though how much of the insides of these pyramids was known in Hellenistic and Roman times is not clear, as we shall see. (The smallest of the Giza three, belonging to King Menkaure (Mycerinus) is also impressively complicated inside, but its considerably smaller scale has always robbed it of stardom.) The Giza pyramids may often feature as the seventh Wonder in trio form (when it is not just a matter of Egyptian pyramids en masse), but it is Khufu's pyramid that draws most of the attention.

The Giza pyramids represent the zenith of the pyramid building in Egypt: they are the best constructed and include the two very largest. They were built over a short span between about 2500 and 2400 BCE. The developmental progress from the Step Pyramid to Khufu's is very clear: through the (now rather collapsed) pyramid of Maidum where an attempt was made to clad a stepped pyramid in smooth-faced casing blocks, to the so-called Bent Pyramid which cautiously changes its angle of slope – smoothly clad – halfway up, and the wholly unsteep Red Pyramid (both at Dahshur, between Sakkara and Giza and both apparently belonging to Khufu's father Snofru). The Bent Pyramid does prefigure, in its many passages and elaborate anti-theft precautions, the unfathomable complexity of the Great Pyramid's interior.

It is rather telling that, of all the Seven Wonders, it should be the oldest alone that substantially survives till today. This situation offers an immediate clue to the truly alien quality (even for the Greeks and Romans) of the world which created the pyramids of Egypt. To have been able to build such prodigious monuments in cut stone, with so little of the sort of technology enjoyed by ourselves or even the Romans and Greeks, demonstrates at once that

Not the Giza pyramids, but a nearby (and slightly later) group, as soberly pictured in the early 20th century series of illustrations of the Seven Wonders

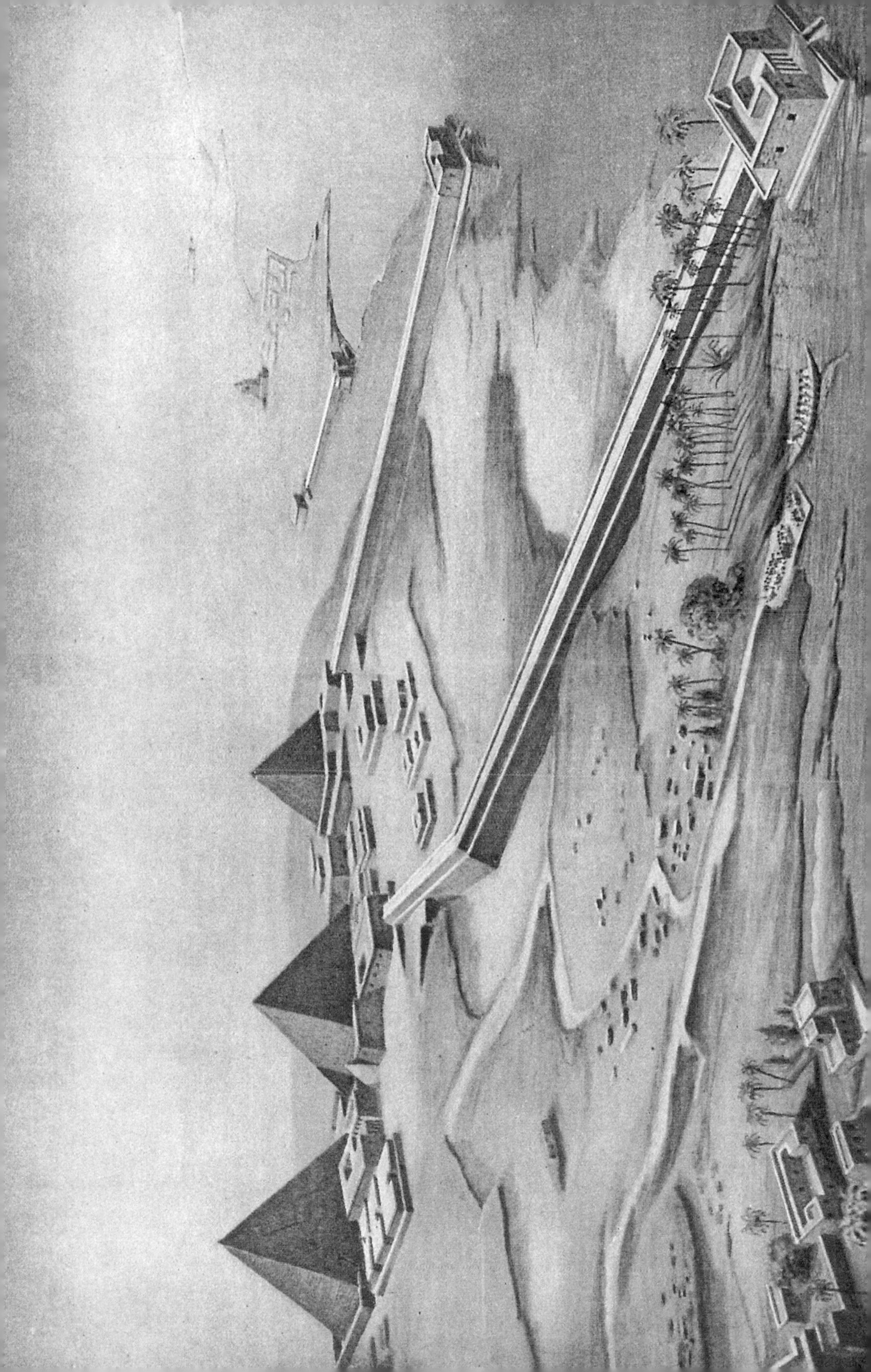

very different social and ideological circumstances applied. Philo, whether in the second century BCE or the fourth century CE, acknowledged that the pyramids were scarcely buildable in his world as well as witnessing to the still smoothly-faced exteriors of the Giza group in his time. Of course, the labours of slaves went into the creation of all the other Wonders of the Ancient World at some stage or another, however much the design and decoration were in the hands of artists and professionals. But even with plentiful slave labour, the Hellenistic world put up nothing to begin to match the enormity – in terms of invested labour as well as size – of the pyramids at Giza. And at the pyramids of Egypt's Old Kingdom (when all the major pyramids were built) we may reasonably doubt that slaves were used at all. Slavery in the formal and legal sense in which it existed as civilisation progressed in later days was not a prominent part of the Egyptian Old Kingdom scene.

We might conclude that there was a sort of servitude of mind in Old Kingdom Egypt that could bring the common folk to labour so hard on behalf of their rulers on what may look like vainglorious productions to us. But such a view would hardly do justice to the force of Old Kingdom ideology, in which kings were quite closely related to God and labour on their tombs was all to the good of the Cosmos. The kings' role in righteously governing the land of Egypt and their god-like status in the after-life justified the construction of their great monumental tombs overlooking the irrigated fields of the Nile Valley from their commanding positions on the desert's edge. A socio-economic benefit of this ideology, and in turn a support for it, came in the form of seasonal employment for a huge workforce originally built up to cut irrigation ditches and plant crops to exploit the Nile's annual flood – what better way to keep that workforce gainfully employed out of the farming season than to occupy it with building such wonderful expressions of state solidarity as the pyramids?

How far the Greeks were from apprehending the true character of Old Kingdom Egypt is well illustrated by the stories Herodotus tells of the building of the Giza pyramids: and how far, indeed, were the Egyptians themselves for that matter by the time of Herodotus, in the fifth century BCE, when assorted dragomans at Giza would appear to have fed their Greek visitor some extraordinary tales. For instance, that Khufu had set his own daughter up in prostitution to help build his pyramid when he was strapped for cash – each customer was to contribute a stone towards the edifice in payment for her services. Pliny some 500 years later took his cue from this curious tale and reported his amazement that the smallest of the Giza pyramids similarly owed its erection to immoral earnings. Pliny thought the pyramids in general a witness to the folly and ostentation of kings. We may reflect that all manifestations of ideology from every time and place are apt to look foolish to those who do not share their presumptions, and the more laborious they are the more empty they look. On this score, only the Pharos lighthouse emerges as something truly wonderful from the ancient wonder lists, as being actually practically useful as well as astounding in design and execution. Not many subsequent wonders of the world fare so well by these standards, either.

But by virtue of the ambition of their concept and construction, the pyramids of Egypt and especially the Giza trio remain truly wonderful and would be so as products of any age in the entire history of the human race. With only the simplest of technical means, but with that large and well-disciplined (if only seasonally available) workforce, the Old Kingdom architects were able to orientate and cut the foundation platforms of the pyramids to an impressive degree of accuracy. Water-filled trenches in the limestone of the Giza plateau facilitated levelling of the site; plumb lines and observations of the circling stars at night permitted the layout of the sides of the planned pyramids with near total precision as to alignment with the cardinal points. Hammering with hard stones and cutting with sand-assisted copper saws, breaking rock with fires and cold dousings, splitting stone with water-swollen wedges, dragging blocks (the smallest weigh several tonnes) over rollers or in wooden cradles up sand ramps, lifting them with counterweights and manoeuvring them with long levers: these were the techniques with which the pyramids were created.

While the technology may have been simple, but very ingeniously applied, the design of the pyramids was often complex inside – particularly in cases like the Bent Pyramid at Dahshur and the Great Pyramid at Giza where there were several interior chambers, shafts and traps built into their construction as it progressed. The architectural planning, and surely detailed drawing which, of course, does not survive, that went into such monuments is quite staggering and clearly establishes the sophistication and cleverness of the designers. At Giza, beside the Great Pyramid, there are trial cuttings with intersecting shafts and corridors that look like architectural experiments or perhaps demonstration pieces to familiarise the workforce with what they were going to have to build. The true wonder of the pyramids could be said to reside in their design, and in the logistics of realising that design. (In overall charge at the Great Pyramid was a relative of Khufu's named Hemon.)

The resulting constructions were primarily tombs and it is clear that, however powerful the ideology of righteous kingship was, the threat of robbery was also ever present. We may suppose that there are always plenty of people whom any amount of ideology cannot constrain, and a good thing too in the long run. Khufu's own mother's tomb had been robbed, for the precious metals and jewels its appointments included, and Khufu and his architects went to extraordinary (but ultimately unavailing) lengths to try to secure his own rich burial. The long sloping shaft that leads down to his first chosen resting place hewn in the rock under his pyramid was no doubt intended to be plugged by a series of blocks chuted down it from an exterior ramp. When a change of plan led to the creation of another burial chamber high inside the fabric of the pyramid, an interior ramp in the so-called grand gallery of the monument was intended to serve the same purpose, delivering blocks back towards the narrower entrance corridor of the pyramid. (Some of these are still in place in their final blocking position, since entry into the pyramid in the ninth century CE was effected by hacking another tunnel round them.)

A third design saw Khufu's burial chamber moved higher still inside his pyramid, at the top of the gallery and protected by stone portcullises lowered into position by the departing burial party, before the triggering of the chute of blocks into the passage connecting the gallery to the area of the pyramid's entrance. The burial crew were evidently furnished – whether with the knowledge and consent of Khufu and his architects or not – with an escape route rather roughly cut down from the gallery to the lower passage leading to the first, underground burial chamber. This may well have been the Achilles' heel of the whole anti-theft endeavour, and the route by which robbers (in league with the burial crew?) were able to enter and loot Khufu's tomb within no time at all of his funeral.

Most of the limestone of the Giza pyramids was quarried on site, with finer material for the facing brought across from the other side of the Nile and granite components rafted down from Upper Egypt. The Sphinx which accompanies the Khafre pyramid, and stands like a guardian to the whole Giza necropolis, was carved out of a knoll left behind by the on-site quarrying. The pyramids had temples immediately before them and further ones down the slope of the Giza escarpment, connected by covered causeways which impressed Herodotus as much as the pyramids themselves. The so-called valley temples fronted onto canals linked to the Nile by which the deceased kings' bodies were brought to Giza for mummification and interment. These temples are in ruins now and the superstructures of the causeways are gone. A good deal of damage was probably done at Giza within a few centuries of the building of the pyramids there, during the relatively lawless First Intermediate Period at the end of the Old Kingdom.

Herodotus is a witness to the continued survival of the magnificent causeway of Khufu's pyramid in the fifth century BCE, when the Giza trio was already about 2000 years old. In his day, probably only the descending corridor that leads to the Great Pyramid's abandoned first-stage deep burial chamber was open. (He swallowed some extravagant stuff from his local guides about what was under the Great Pyramid.) The rough shaft leading up from the descending corridor to the gallery high inside the pyramid may or may not have been known to the local priesthood by this date, but Herodotus knows nothing of it. We can be pretty sure that Khufu and all his goods were long gone, the portcullis leading into his burial chamber smashed through perhaps almost as long as a couple of thousand years before.

In the late first century BCE, Diodorus can report no consensus as to the age of the Giza pyramids (between 1000 and 3500 years, he thinks) and Strabo knows no more of the Great Pyramid's interior than Herodotus did, though he intriguingly records that a movable slab (pivoted, evidently) closed the entrance to the pyramid in his time: the raising of this slab allowed entrance into the corridor descending to the original – and, incidentally, unfinished – subterranean burial chamber. Whether this ingenious slab was part of the original design is now impossible to know.

And so, in Greek and Roman times, the Giza pyramids were already – halfway through from their own time to ours – something of a mystery and not very well-known inside (in the case of Khafre and Menkaure, very likely not known at all). Their associated temples were already ruined or, the ones at the bottom of their causeways, swamped in sand and built over. The causeways were part-robbed of their coverings, at the very least, and the whole locale so ruined, rebuilt, added-to and altered as to convey – along with the presence of a variety of native and foreign cults and their agents – the general effect of a fairground, part tourist attraction and part abode of mountebanks and priestcraft. But still, the pyramids themselves were relatively untouched: certainly

The Great Pyramid, with temples and causeway: behind it, the pyramid of Khafre to which the Sphinx belongs. Insets show a possible ramp constructional method and the puzzling interior features of the Great Pyramid

they still wore their shining outer coats of finely finished smooth cladding stones, which must have given them an altogether different look from the one they sport today. Just a glimpse of how they once appeared is afforded by the remaining courses of cladding that the Khafre pyramid retains at its top, which still shine with the right angle of sunlight reflected off them. (When Herodotus, with seeming absurdity, avers that the pyramids were built from the top down, according to his Egyptian informants, we may detect a memory or surmise of the dressing of the smooth casing of the monuments, which must have been achieved in that way.)

The Ancient World knew nothing to compare with the Giza pyramids for bulk and antiquity: the Great Pyramid of Khufu would remain the world's tallest construction until modern times. Robbed of its top few courses and of the spectacularly carved granite pyramidion, with the orb of the sun-god on it, that once graced its peak (to go by other pyramids), it still stands some 140 m high and covers some 5.4 hectares of ground plan, with perhaps more than two million blocks of between 2 and 15 tonnes inside it (built around a pre-existing low knoll of rock, as a matter of fact). Herodotus says it took twenty years to build, which may or may not be the case – Khufu reigned for twenty-three years. Probably pyramid building in Old Kingdom Egypt was a rolling project, not entirely synchronised with kings' reigns, in line with its socio-economic as well as ideological purposes. Certainly the Great Pyramid belonged to Khufu, however, as tradition always said it did – his name has been found in highly inaccessible places inside it, written on some blocks by workmen in the course of its construction.

There are many mysteries in the Great Pyramid at Giza, as is bound to be the case with such a complex monument built over a fairly long period with several major changes of plan as well as all the inevitable minor ones, robbed in some ingenious way in remote antiquity, then subject to a long cycle of half-hearted renovations alternating with neglect, sometimes partly open to visitors and sometimes blocked up, finally penetrated – after its entrance was lost sight of altogether – by the crudest of means in the ninth century CE, and since then explored and tinkered with by a multitude of scholars, visitors and assorted crackpots.

The roughly cut shaft that might have been the burial party's escape route and/or the robbers' first means of entry is one such mystery, since we cannot know who made it and on whose authority nor whether it was officially blocked up at the time of the funeral or at some time afterwards. Pairs of narrow shafts that were built into the design first of the so-called Queen's Chamber (but unfinished there) and then into the King's Chamber above it are further mysteries, as to what they were for and where, in the latter case, they emerge on the exterior slopes of the monument. They appear to show significant astronomical alignments of 4500 years ago, to do with the constellation of Orion (which the Egyptians saw as Osiris, god of resurrection) and the star Sirius (Isis, consort of Osiris). One of them recently aroused much interest when a tiny motorised video camera was able to reach a deliberate blockage in the shaft, posing the question of what there might be on the other side. (Actually, it can't be much as this shaft is only about 175 mm square.)

From time to time people announce that they have 'proved' the existence of further chambers in the Khufu pyramid, without being able to physically explore them, and attempts have been made to detect by high-tech methods similar unknown chambers in the Khafre pyramid too, without signal success. Enthusiasm for such secret chambers goes back a long way: Herodotus talks of waters beneath the pyramids and an artificial island under Khufu's; and it was the lure of secret chambers full of riches, either gold and jewels or some sort of abstruse knowledge, that lured the Arabs into their brutal rediscovery of the corridors and rooms in the upper part of the Great Pyramid – as we shall see in our final chapter. The Greek and Roman tourists, who had read up on the pyramids as one of the Wonders of their world, knew nothing of the upper features that today's tourists can visit with the benefit of electric light. But they certainly knew a wonder when they saw one, as we too cannot fail to do with the pyramids of Egypt.

The Giza trio constituted the peak of pyramid building in Egypt, but they were by no means the last of Egyptian pyramids. During the remaining couple of dynasties of the Old Kingdom after the time of Khufu, Khafre and Menkaure, succeeding kings – for the most part – provided themselves with pyramids along the desert's edge, between Giza and Sakkara. They were not so large as the Giza pyramids and they were by no means so well built, so that the remains of some of them – mere shapeless piles of stones – scarcely look like pyramids at all. These piles started life as very impressive monuments made of fine quality cladding over rubble-filled interiors: they were made on the cheap, in other words; and when their outer layers were robbed, the interiors collapsed. They must have looked wonderful once, too, and their surrounding complexes were if anything grander and more ornate than those of the Giza group, but they lacked the staying power. When the Old Kingdom ended in something like anarchy in about 2200 BCE, the great age of pyramid building as tombs for kings was over though the pyramid form never vanished from Egyptian architecture. It is not just that a pyramid makes a rather convenient way of building high on a massive scale (a convenience that helps to account for pyramid building in other times and places than Old Kingdom Egypt): the image had significance for Egyptian religion as a symbolic reminder of the first mound of earth to emerge from the waters of chaos at the beginning of time and as the peak over which the Sun's rays reached down to Earth each day, like a ladder the dead king might climb to heaven.

It is easy to see how the Hellenistic wonder list compilers, the centre of whose world was in Alexandria only about 200 km north of Giza, could hardly fail to include the pyramids among their Seven Wonders. If the pyramids had been sited anywhere at all in the known world of the Greeks and Romans let alone so close to home, their sheer size and audacity of construction would have earned them their place. (And however old they were, they belonged to a still extant civilisation with a continuity of culture going back for thousands of years.) What of the wider world the Greeks and Romans did not know? What products of humanity of an age comparable with the pyramids of Egypt or older than them, might the list-makers have included if they had known of them? From the point of view of Greek and Roman artistic sensibility and taste, not many – as we keep on having to observe! The Greeks and Romans may have had their intellectual curiosity aroused by one or two things, if they could have known how old they were, but in the absence of such knowledge, only grandeur of scale and ambition would have counted. On that score, the Great Bath of Mohenjo-daro in the Indus Valley, which was built at about the same time as the Giza pyramids, might have impressed along the same lines as the fabled Gardens, if it had survived and come to the attention of the Hellenistic world.

It used to be thought that the Egyptians were the world's first builders in hewn stone and certainly they could claim to be the first to build with regularly cut and highly finished components. But the megalithic building tradition of western Europe, to which Stonehenge belongs, well predates the Egyptians' use of shaped stone. Stonehenge, as we have seen, reached its final form a few centuries after the building of the Giza pyramids, but it was started half-a-millenium before them. Some of the west European megalithic tombs go back to nearly 5000 years BCE and the highly elaborate stone-built temples of Malta and Gozo also predate the building of the pyramids. Complex interior layouts were built into these temples of between about 3600 and 2500 BCE, made out of limestone blocks with limestone facing slabs. There are signs that they were roofed in wood with stairs to the top of them; they contained altars and slabs carved with elaborate designs including running spirals. Barbarous they may have been by comparison with the Temple of Artemis at Ephesus or the Temple of Zeus at Olympia, but most Greeks would surely have been amazed to hear that they were 2000 to 3000 years older than those and older even than the pyramids.

Older still by far are the walls and towers of Jericho – not of course the walls that Joshua is alleged to have tumbled with trumpet blasts in about 1200 BCE, but the much older defences of a small settlement of the earliest days of the farming way of life, built in around 8000 BCE. The loose stone construction of these walls and rather grand towers (one of them has an interior staircase) only impresses when we realise how old and how innovatory they are: they are a wonder of the world because they reveal, thanks to archaeological excavation, the achievement of some of the earliest exponents of the settled, farming economy developed after the close of the last ice age.

If we venture back into that last ice age itself, we may contemplate the staggering cave art of the west European Old Stone Age hunters and gatherers who painted and engraved the animals (mostly) of their harsh but abundant world between about 30,000 and 12,000 BCE. What the Greeks and Romans would have made of all this, we can only guess. Probably some examples of this ancient art did occasionally come to light among Gallic or Iberian citizens of the Roman empire, but with no means of dating it or relating it to the very different world in which it was created, it would have figured as only a short-lived and irrelevant mystery. The philosophers, at least, might have been interested to know that previous cycles of human existence had thrown up such wonders, 10,000 or 20,000 years before the Egyptian pyramids which were the oldest things they knew.

AFTERMATHS

Part of a frieze from the Mausoleum, on show in the British Museum

Chapter 9
AFTERMATHS

THE pyramids of Egypt are mostly still with us: the Giza trio, despite extensive damage and robbery, look as though they will last for ever. It seems clear that their smooth casings were still in place well into the Common Era – they were robbed away to help build the Arab city of Cairo. (An ambitious sheikh of the thirteenth century CE embarked on a project to demolish Menkaure's pyramid altogether: its present reasonably good shape after all his efforts only shows how difficult such a task would be.) As we have seen, the Great Pyramid of Khufu was partly open in Roman times, with access through the original entrance into the long corridor that descends into the unfinished original burial chamber in the bedrock below the pyramid. By the time of the Arab conquest of Egypt in the seventh century CE, sight of that original entrance (and what it led to) seems to have been lost, so that al-Mamun – son of Harun al-Rashid of the Arabian Nights – had to force his way into the Great Pyramid in the ninth century, apparently in search of treasure though a quest for lost knowledge has also been suggested.

Al-Mamun's team burrowed their way into the fabric of the monument, eventually encountering the top of the descending corridor where it intersected with another corridor rising at an angle into the body of the pyramid. This ascending corridor was blocked with stone plugs, which the Arabs carved their way around till they gained full access into the ascending corridor and thereby the grand gallery and the high burial chamber of Khufu, with his empty sarcophagus inside it. A story has it that al-Mamun, to avoid the dangerous disappointment of his men after so much labour, smuggled a bogus treasure into the pyramid and kept them quiet with that. We can conclude that the original treasure of Khufu, together with his mummy, was long since broken up and looted away, very likely in Old Kingdom times or in the First Intermediate Period after that.

Quite when and how the various bits of quite extensive damage seen in the Great Pyramid's interior were done is hard to say now: some of it early on, some of it at different times since al-Mamun's entry, most likely. The rough shaft from the lower end of the gallery down to the descending corridor was apparently found and lost again more than once before final clearance in the nineteenth century CE. The exploration of the pressure-relieving chambers above the King's Chamber was achieved only in the nineteenth century, and of course exploration goes on today – as with the robot cameras up the narrow shafts that lead out from the chambers.

The Giza pyramids have always aroused rather wild speculation, as though any account of their origins and purpose except for the plain fact of their being tombs would be better than facing the truth about them. In the Middle Ages, they were the granaries of Joseph during his brilliant Egyptian career according to the Bible, despite their obvious solid impracticability for grain storage in quantity. In the nineteenth century, they were – the complex Great Pyramid at least – prodigious encoded records of all history and prophecies for the divinely-inspired future of the human race. On the other hand, Flinders Petrie, the father of systematic archaeology in Egypt, cut his teeth on the Great Pyramid in the nineteenth century, though he had been taken there to bolster the metrological theories of a Biblically-fixated crackpot who happened to be Scotland's Astronomer Royal.

The pyramids, as we have seen, are the only sights of the standard list to have substantially survived into modern times. One wonders how long the Hanging Gardens can possibly have lasted from the time of their construction around 600 BCE, with or without the attentions of Xerxes. They are mentioned by several sources as though still existing in the time of Alexander, at least, nearly three centuries after their creation. That seems a tall order for the sort of bitumened wooden platforms that Philo entertains. But perhaps a few centuries' survival is not too implausible if we regard Philo's details as late conjectures, and picture something more like a stone-built series of terraces watered from a reservoir and shielded by walls, located near the Euphrates. However long they lasted, it is worth recalling that no Babylonian source ever mentions them at all either as being established in the first place, as being there as a feature of the city or as being derelict and

demolished. And likewise, archaeology cannot be said to have found proof positive of their existence in Babylon to this day, nor a definite location for them.

The fate of the Temple of Artemis at Ephesus is better known. The cult statue of the goddess was famous for having twice saved Ephesus from despoliation, but it did not save the city in 262 CE when ships of the Goths, sailing from the Crimea, sacked city and temple together. The temple was rebuilt, however, in time to suffer earthquake damage in the fourth century CE. The temple and its cult had survived the denunciation of Paul of Tarsus in the first century CE, but it ran into real trouble with the Christian patriarch of Constantinople in 401 CE.

Robbery of its fabric began and a limekiln was set up, to exploit the pagan temple for Christian building purposes. Some of its surviving statuary was shipped off to Constantinople to join a collection (with some even more illustrious pieces, as we shall see) of antique art there. The Christians were evidently pretty wary of Artemis, that great goddess with such deep and ancient roots in this part of the world. They chiselled their crosses onto everything they couldn't remove or render down: and they set about appropriating the cult of Artemis to their own version of the Great Mother. The Virgin Mary was now supposed to have lived, with the author of the fourth of the Christians' gospels, on St John's Hill close to Ephesus – and it was to that location that the citizenry removed themselves after another earthquake in 614 CE made Ephesus insecure. The river here was always prone to silting and, with farmlands abandoned in the hinterland to loose their untilled soil, the harbour had to be closed and what was left of city and temple after the attentions of Christians and then Moslems went under the silts and floods.

The Artemis temple was one of the first items of lost antiquity to be deliberately sought out by archaeological means. In the 1860s, a British railway engineer working out of Smyrna, whose name was John Turtle Wood, began to explore the presumed site of

Ephesus with little but the remarks of the classical authors to go by. It was a long job, with the outer wall of the temple only coming to light after six years of digging up various other parts of the ancient city, and many more years needed to uncover as much as he could of it. By 1873 Wood knew there had been at least three builds of the temple on the site. Another excavator in the early part of the twentieth century established that there had been five phases of temple there, getting down into waterlogged deposits that Wood couldn't work in and finding many of the votive materials we reviewed in the Ephesus chapter. Modern excavations have greatly advanced our knowledge of the site, but still little more than one re-erected column marks the site of this ancient Wonder for the modern visitor: the desecrators robbed away and worked their limekilns all too well.

The site of the Temple of Zeus at Olympia, and indeed the whole complex of shrines and facilities of the games, suffered a similar fate to that of the city of Ephesus, when the river Alpheus changed its course and – helped by a fire in 425 CE – put paid to nearly the entire Olympic site under a covering of mud and sand. But as a matter of fact, by the time of that turn of fate, the statue of Zeus was already gone from his temple. Its creator, by the way, met a sad end not long after achieving his masterpiece – Phidias died in prison, maybe by execution or just plain murder, either in Olympia itself (where he was accused of stealing gold meant for the Zeus statue's cloak) or in Athens where his enemies were many, at all events in 432 BCE.

His wonderful statue was to outlast him by nearly 900 years. Naturally, its vicissitudes were considerable during the long time of its existence. Pausanias mentions four support columns under its throne that are not shown on any of the coins of Elis that are more or less contemporary with its making: perhaps they had needed to be added by the time of the Roman Empire because the thing was just so heavy. We know that the statue had to be mended in the second century BCE on account of cracking of the ivory, and in that same century there was earthquake damage to both temple and statue, to be followed by restoration work. The emperor Caligula had work started to remove the statue away to Rome, but Suetonius reports that a great cackle of laughter emanating from the Zeus caused Caligula's scaffolding to collapse and his workmen to run for their lives, whereupon the local Roman governor rather bravely told Caligula he just couldn't have it.

What a pagan emperor could not overcome, the Christian emperors could. Constantine ordered the stripping of the ample gold of the Zeus statue. In 391 CE, Theodosius banished the pagan cults on the urgings of the church and the whole site of Olympia fell into neglect, along with the end of the Olympic Games. The place began to be robbed and the site of the workshops of Phidias became a church, following the plan of his building. A court chamberlain of Theodosius, however, was a collector of all sorts of antiquities from the destroyed pagan sites and, early in the fifth century CE, the gold-deprived statue of Zeus was taken away to Constantinople, to join – among much else – that statuary we mentioned as being sent off from the Artemis temple. But this was not the long-term saving of the Zeus statue, for a great fire later on in the same century destroyed the palace in which the pagan loot was lodged and Zeus went up with it. So perished what everyone in the Ancient World agreed was a surpassingly beautiful realisation of the classical Greeks' idea of the father of the Gods. But rather as Artemis was incorporated into the Virgin Mary and the sun-god in the guise of Alexander gave his face to the early iconography of Christ, so the Zeus head became the model for the Christians' god in his strongest and sternest expression as the Pantocrator, ruler over all things.

The Mausoleum at Halicarnassus never really disappeared from ken. Indeed it appears to have stood in fairly good order until the thirteenth century CE, when an earthquake brought down its upper part: the chariot group, certainly, and probably part of the pyramid above the columns. Neglect and decay proceeded to take their toll, but it must have remained an imposing wreck into the fifteenth century – until some people with a use for its conveniently collected and pre-shaped raw materials came along. In 1494 CE, the Knights of St John set about re-fortifying their castle at Bodrum, as Halicarnassus is now known, and there was the part-ruined Mausoleum to supply their needs. They especially favoured the green volcanic stones from the core of the ancient structure for building purposes, mostly smashing up the fine marble casings, friezes and statuary to burn for mortar. They worked fast and by the end of the first quarter of the sixteenth century, pretty well everything had been disposed of down to the foundations (as we have seen, even the Knights made a bit of decorative use of some of the sculptures and fragments of friezes that took their fancy).

In 1522, the Knights found the tomb chamber under the now demolished Mausoleum and took a look into it. According to an account of 1581, they found an underground room crammed with sculpture which may in fact have been simply tumbled debris of sculptures thrown down from the Mausoleum's higher stages during the thirteenth century earthquake. Their wonder at this collection of superb sculpture did not hold them back for long from smashing it up as they had done with everything else and burning it for lime. They also found the tomb chamber itself, of which they decided to postpone further exploration until the next day. This turned out to have been a mistake on the Knights' part, for when they returned they found the burial chamber comprehensively wrecked by – as they concluded – pirates who had got wind of the discovery and made an overnight raid to carry off its treasures. And in fact modern excavations have found fragments of the lid of the burial place of the remains of King Mausolus and spangles from the cloth in which his ashes were wrapped. It's a moot point whether the treasures of the tomb would have fared any better in the hands of the Knights than in those of the pirates. The sacrifice of the still impressive ruins of

the Mausoleum to re-fortify their military base was all rather in vain, in any case, as the Knights were soon seen off by the Turks.

All that survived into later centuries were the foundations of the Mausoleum, traces of the staircase into the subterranean tomb and smashed architectural remains lying about the site – and it was occasional reports by European travellers of these remnants that prompted excavation in the nineteenth century, bringing some fine pieces to the British Museum, and revealing the extent of the Knights' vandalism in their attempt to build against the Turks' big guns. A once magnificent sculpture of a mounted Persian rider, for instance, had been sledge-hammered to pieces to burn for lime. But archaeological excavations were able to dig down into soil deeper than the Knights had cared to delve, bringing back to light such items as steps from the pyramid top of the monument and architrave beams that once linked the columns beneath the pyramid. The British Museum's best relics of the Mausoleum are, of course, the great statues of Mausolus and his queen (if such they really be) and the horse from the chariot group of the very peak of the monument, together with the lion that was removed from the Knights' castle.

There's nothing like all that to show for the Colossus of Rhodes now: in fact, there's nothing at all. The wonderful statue lay where it fell after the earthquakes of the late third century BCE – for about nine centuries, a continuing wonder in its overthrown state. The Arabs looted Rhodes in 654 CE and took the wreckage of the Colossus (probably removing the broken-off feet and calves on their pedestal at the same time). It wasn't at all difficult to break up an already smashed monument that had been cast in separate pieces in the first place. The story goes that in Asia Minor the Arabs sold the scrap (to finance a fight among themselves) to a Jew who conveyed it into Syria on 900 camels, at which point we naturally lose sight of it for ever. It must all have come to a mundane end.

The Pharos of Alexandria seems to have gone on in use into Arab

Statues generally thought to model Artemis and Mausolus, that once stood high among the columns of the Mausoleum

times. As we have seen, the Arab conquerors of Egypt built a mosque on its top, which is shown in the Venetian mosaic and mentioned by Arab writers. Bad damage was done to the Pharos in 956 CE as a result of an earthquake (and perhaps that was when the mosque was added, during repairs). There were further earthquakes in 1303 and 1323. Ibn Battuta says the lighthouse was partially in ruins in 1326 and very much the worse for wear in 1349 when he saw it again, by which time it was no longer possible to get up to the entrance door in its lower section. Another earthquake, in 1375, shook the already battered monument to its foundations. In the late fifteenth century, a massive fort (again to oppose the Turks) was built on the site and out of the remains of the ruined Pharos. The island on which the lighthouse stood, and where the fort still stands, has long since been joined to the city of Alexandria – first by the mole that could be sometimes flooded over but now by solid ground. But a good deal of old Alexandria is now under the sea, including perhaps the tomb of Alexander himself. Underwater exploration continues to bring up impressive remains of the Greek and Roman city, among them a statue of Isis Pharia – the old Egyptian goddess in her special guise as mistress of the island from which the Pharos once radiated its fiery beams.

'Philo of Byzantium', whether writing in the second century BCE or the fourth century CE, remarks that 'Everyone has heard of all the Seven Wonders of the World, but few people have seen them all for themselves. To do that, you have to go abroad to Persia, cross the Euphrates, go into Egypt, sojourn among the Elians in Greece, travel to Halicarnassus in Caria, sail to Rhodes, see Ephesus in Ionia. Only by travelling the world and wearing yourself out with the journeying will your desire to see all the Wonders of the World be met, and by the time you've done all that you will be old and well nigh dead.' It's a neat conceit (if a vast exaggeration), but the Seven Wonders were always really a literary concoction, intended for armchair satisfactions. By the fourth century CE, the Hanging Gardens cannot have been visible at all, even if the city walls of Babylon were still partly in place. The fully-functioning Pharos wasn't on Philo's list, but the Colossus was a rather ageing and, as far as the iron component of its armature was concerned, a rather rusty ruin. The Mausoleum must still have looked pretty good, but the Artemis Temple was never to be the same again after the Goths' assault of 262. The Statue of Zeus at Olympia was still going strong and the Pyramids, of course, were the same as ever – it's hard to think now that anything but the explosion of the sun and the burn-up of the earth will ever put paid to them.

But in the time of 'Philo's' account of the Seven Wonders, they were really becoming something even more in the nature of a pure idea, for everyone, than they had been before for most of the readership that would never visit them. The idea could outlive the details, with new items coming onto lists and older ones being jostled out. The palace of Cyrus at Ecbatana, further east than Babylon, made a brief showing, as did with the same obscure late Roman author of *On the Wonders of the World*, one Ampelius, the Altar of the Giants at Pergamum.

From time to time the temple complexes of Thebes in Upper Egypt gained that city an ephemeral place on the lists, and a legendary labyrinth, partly inspired by the Theban temples and partly by other Egyptian funerary monuments, occasionally figured too. Some Christian writers wanted to be rid of the pagan temples and substituted Noah's Ark and Solomon's Temple for the Zeus Statue and Temple of Artemis. Cosmas of Jerusalem preferred Hagia Sophia in Constantinople over Solomon's Temple, and his choice has at least the merit of actually existing (it's the Great Mosque of Istanbul today). Gregory of Tours, who favoured Solomon's Temple, also included the Capitol of Rome and an elusive theatre at Heraclea apparently in the region of the Black Sea, and he it was who put the Pharos on the list at the end of the sixth century, but he left out the Pyramids and Gardens, along with Zeus and Artemis. (Pliny had recounted the Pharos, but not made it one of the Seven Wonders as such.) A century after Gregory, Bede of Jarrow espoused the Colossus, the Temple at Ephesus, Gregory's Capitol and stadium at Heracleia, as well as Pharos, plus a fabulous statue of Alexander's horse Bellerophon at Smyrna and a bathhouse at Tyana.

Gregory also produced, in Christian spirit, a list of wonders not made by the hand of man but by nature at God's direction: these included such grandeurs as the sun and moon, the movements of the sea and the germinations of nature alongside, more bathetically, a volcano in Sicily and a warm-water spring in cold Grenoble. To fully establish his Dark Ages credentials, Gregory also listed the phoenix, that mythical bird that was supposed to be resurrected out of its own ashes. Wonder-listing was thus starting to show its distance in time and spirit from the Hellenistic world in which it had been first developed. The modern world has found no difficulty in adding things like Niagara Falls, the Empire State Building, Mount Rushmore's presidential faces and space rockets to the wonder-listing habit.

Showing what the Wonders of the Ancient World might actually have looked like (rather than just reading, in often rather vague terms, about them) only began to be attempted in Renaissance times. It isn't an easy task even today, with benefit of archaeology, to come up with some concrete depiction that has the required degree of basis in known fact and general plausibility. The artists of Renaissance times, and frankly right up to the last century, had less to go on than we do and more prejudices (or at least we like to think so) about what ancient monuments could possibly have looked like. The first depictions of the Wonders of the Ancient World seem to have been drawn by Cesare Cesariano as embellishment to footnotes for his translation in 1521 of the Roman architectural writer Vitruvius: his Mausoleum, for example, is more or less a Renaissance church with a soldier-saint's statue on top.

Martaen van Heemskerck's slightly later and better known engravings are pretty fanciful creations of which it may be said that not one of them bears any resemblance at all to what the real Wonders can have been. The case is particularly bad with the Pyramids, which look like obelisks, and the Artemis Temple, which has no resemblance to a classical temple at all. In the early eighteenth century, Fischer von Ehrlach did rather better with Pyramids, Pharos, Babylon and even Mausoleum and Artemisium. But he still went rather badly wrong with the Colossus – like everyone else he wanted to see it astride the harbour mouth – and with the Zeus Temple at Olympia, oddly enough, where his attention to what the ancient writers said led him to underplay the real character of classical temples with which he was familiar.

The lush peak of Wonder reconstructing was achieved in the early twentieth century with the rosy paintings featured in an American part-work, since widely reproduced and contributing most significantly to the public idea of what the Seven Wonders of the Ancient World were really like. They are in several cases widely divergent from what the Wonders can possibly ever have been, particularly so with the Hanging Gardens, and the same might be said of Salvador Dali's ventures into wonderland in the 1950s – like the striking Colossus featured on our cover. But all these highly coloured depictions from the past, taken along with archaeologically up-to-date and more sober reconstructions, like those by Mac Dowdy in this book, do help us to realise the wonderfulness of their originals in the mind's eye. And after all, the Seven Wonders of the Ancient World were always something of a dream for most of the people who heard and read about them and all the writers who described them meant to make an impression of something out of the ordinary, more than usually wonderful.

FURTHER READING

THE CLASSICAL AUTHORS

Diodorus Siculus *Library of History*
Herodotus *Histories*
Manetho *Egyptian Memoirs*
Pausanias *Guide to Greece*
Philo of Byzantium *Seven Sights of the World*
Pliny (the Elder) *Natural History*
Strabo *Geography*
Vitruvius *Ten Books of Architecture*

The best way to read (most of) these authors is in the Loeb editions published by Harvard University Press, with Greek or Latin on one side and English translation on the other. Manetho is quoted in Josephus and Philo's brief account of the Wonders is translated in Romer, see below.

BOOKS ABOUT THE SEVEN WONDERS

Ashley, M. (1980) *The Seven Wonders of the World*, Glasgow: Fontana.

Clayton, P. and Price, M.J., Eds. (1990) *The Seven Wonders of the Ancient World*, London: Routledge.

Hammerton, J.A., Ed. (1924) *Wonders of the Past*, part-work published in New York.

Romer, J. and E. (1995) *The Seven Wonders of the World: a History of the Modern Imagination*, London: Thames and Hudson Ltd.

Scarre, C., Ed. (1999) *The Seventy Wonders of the Ancient World*, London: Thames and Hudson Ltd.

BOOKS ABOUT THE CLASSICAL WORLD

Boardman, J., Griffin J. and Murray, O. (1986) *The Oxford History of the Classical World*, Oxford University Press.

Hornblower, S. and Spawforth, A., Eds. (1996) *The Oxford Classical Dictionary*, Oxford and New York: Oxford University Press.

Levi, Peter (1980) *Atlas of the Greek World*, Oxford: Phaidon Press Ltd.

Onians, J. (1979) *Art and Thought in the Hellenistic Age*, London: Thames and Hudson Ltd.

BOOKS ABOUT THE ARCHAEOLOGICAL BACKGROUND

Bahn, P.G. (2000) *The Atlas of World Archaeology*, London: Time-Life Books.

Scarre, C., Ed. (1988) *Past Worlds – The Time Atlas of Archaeology*, London: Times Books Ltd.

Sherrat, C., Ed. (1980) *The Cambridge Encyclopedia of Archaeology*, Cambridge University Press.

Whitehouse, R. and Wilkins, J. (1986) *The Making of Civilisation*, London: Collins.

INDEX